If I'm SO Successful

- How come I never get to be on

Top?

By Sharon Tieman

✝

EDES PUBLISHING CO.

IF I'M SO SUCCESSFUL - HOW COME I NEVER GET TO BE ON TOP?

By Sharon Tieman

ISBN-13: 978-0-9788010-6-9
ISBN-10: 0-9788010-6-7

Made in the United States of America

TABLE OF CONTENTS

What others are saying about…..
'If I'm SO Successful - How come I never get to be on Top?'

"This book really helped a lot. Sharon's help, advice and opinions gave me the answers that I didn't expect. She is always looking outside the square. Sharon's experience and knowledge in Marketing especially as well as all business dealings stands her above the rest."

-- *Kerry Smith TRIM TONE Weight Loss & Toning Studio. NSW. Australia*

"Thanks so much Sharon for your help negotiating the sale of my first business. After reading this book, your very clear insight into what is important to both parties and how to use this insight to always keep in control of the negotiations made a very stressful time almost fun!"

– *Janet Beckers Niche Partners NSW, Australia. www.nichepartners.biz*

"This book is chock-a-block with practical, immediately use-able marketing tips. I've been in business for 20 years and yet learned a hell of a lot from this book. I can't recommend it highly enough."

-- *Carolyn Dufton Franchise Consultant NSW, Australia. www.franchisingplus.com.au*

"Ever generous with sharing her knowledge, I can see how Sharon has been dubbed "Madam Marketing" by her peers. Sharon's wealth of knowledge comes from years of learning with masters of marketing and practical application in her own businesses."

-- *Ann Rolfe Director, Synergetic People Development Pty Limited www.mentoring-works.com*

"Sharon Tieman is one of the most passionate people I know, especially when it comes to finding a balance between business and family. Being a huge advocate of women in business, she has spent many years coming up with a successful formula to help us all achieve this challenge. While many marketing people are innovative and creative in their marketing campaigns, few can combine this with the financial and business street smarts to make them profitable. Sharon Tieman is this rare combination, she is truly Madame Marketing. I look forward to her next book!"

-- *Lynn Crowe. Director. www.somethingfabulous.com.au*

"In her book Sharon gives some really practical advice on how to be a successful, nurturing mother, and be successful in the business world also. You CAN have it all & still be respected in the morning! She explains how you must first take care of yourself though, so you can take care of everyone, & everything else."

-- *Deanne Apostolou. Dip. Med. Herbalism, Health and Lifestyle Coach. www.looking-fantastic.com*

"If you have just started your own business, are about to or want to take your business to a new level, you need this book. Sharon has filled it with practical and very useful advice. Real common sense. Follow it and you will succeed in creating a profitable business, whether you are male or female."

-- *Toby Marshall. Director. Abacus Recruitment Solutions. www.abacusrecruit.com.au*

"I've read marketing, self-help, positive thinking, body language books. Attended numerous marketing / sales technique seminars, done a copy writing course to help in my chosen field and have been in marketing / sales all my working life. What Sharon has managed to put into these few pages takes most of us a working lifetime to learn. The secrets Sharon shares from her learned insights of being a successful woman in business, a loving and guilt free mother and wife can help you on your way to becoming another Madame Marketing! ...and have some fun along the way!"

-- *Trish Day. HLP Controls Pty Ltd.*

"Sharon tells it like it is for working mothers in business - so get your highlighters out when you read this book. Apart from some important distinctions on what it takes to make your business life easier, Sharon has included some great business tools which pinpoint quickly where you should best spend YOUR time in YOUR business. If only I'd had this book earlier in my business career to realise that you cannot do it all - I tried and learnt the hard way! For anyone in business this practical book will simplify both your business and family life."

-- *Helen Disler*
www.farmingsecrets.com

"Finally! A clear action plan guide to what we can do to get real results in our business. This is a fantastic starting point to uncover the secrets of business success, and I love the real life experiences shared throughout the book. This is a must have book for women who want to avoid overwhelm, and have a reference point and checklists of the essential elements to get sorted. Not only are you on Top, Sharon, you've also ended the 'doing it all myself' syndrome that so many of us girls are experts at! I'll be recommending this book throughout my women's networking groups."

-- *Jo Kefford, The Results Creator –Internet Marketing Solutions, Auckland NZ*
www.resultscreator.com

ABOUT THE AUTHOR

What Secrets?

I am now a mother, wife and business owner. I have been married throughout my business life. I now manage a multi-million dollar business and for the majority of the time, work on it during school hours from my home office.

Which started me thinking. What does success look like for a women or even a mother in business? What does it feel like to be 'on top' in the business world and still be a mother and wife? I could only think of the stereotypical version of success for a man. Great business, the man works long hours, and has a supportive wife who helps maintain the home and family. I was missing a crucial ingredient – a wife!

There have been many studies done about women in the workforce doing the majority of work at home. They still run news stories on the novelty of the "stay at home" Dad. So I suppose being a Mum and running a business must be a novelty too! I have a great husband who helps around the home a lot, but it wasn't always that way.

What's the big deal about mothers in business anyway? Well if it's still such a novelty that they do news stories about it, obviously lots.

My version of success, is still getting to enjoy being a wife, and a mother as well as enjoying the challenges and adrenalin rush I get from business. The thing is, I tried to do it all perfectly and felt like I was an exhausted wreck all the time. I know a lot of women who run businesses and I see them struggle. They struggle with the imbalance of home life and work life. They struggle with the imbalance of being a nurturing mum and a hard faced leader at work. They struggle with finding time for themselves, when there is always something to do in a small business that is of a higher priority. They struggle with the guilt of being a good mum, wife or daughter.

I have been there myself. There are not enough of us who stand up and tell everyone how hard it is and what they can do to find the solutions. We are not the weaker sex; we are the stronger ones - just a little tired right now. I believe as mothers in business we need to know the secrets and shortcuts or we'll fall into exhausted heaps at the end of it all.

I also believe, probably rather idealistically, that more women in business will make a better world. Women are more compassionate and understanding and we don't let our ego get in the way of asking for help. We will only be able to get more women into business by educating ourselves and helping each other.

The education that has helped me the most is not the formal type. My education has been as a result of making loads of mistakes, sometimes costing tens of thousands of dollars. In learning from those experiences, I have learnt that I will always make mistakes. I have also learnt to let them go and to reduce my risks. My great mentor Mal Emery says "cry once – and get on with it". My Dad says, "cut your loses early, the initial pain of a hard decision is short". As women we can beat ourselves up about anything from business to motherhood. Guilt can be common ground.

Over the years I have spent many thousands of dollars on seminars, books and coaching. More costly has been the time I gave up to learn.

Weekends away from my children and time away from catching up with friends. Don't get me wrong, I have no regrets. I just feel that if I knew many years ago, what I know

now, I would have been here a lot sooner. I don't want you to have to go through all that pain, anguish and stress, so the ideas I will give you in this book are the short-cut, fast-track ones which have worked for me.

What I have learnt is about being a mother in business is it's about self correction, not perfection, it's about being really clear about what you want, and what your version of 'success' looks like.

Like many entrepreneurs, I have so much passion for what I do, that I often have to make myself stop and reflect on why I am doing it.

You see, it's an exciting time we live in right now. It's the information age. Never have so many people been so generous with their knowledge and made it so accessible via the World Wide Web. It's the perfect time to find what suits you.

There are many ways to be right. Thankfully from my love of business, I took on many mentors, enjoyed many books and seminars and was able to find a business lifestyle that suited my values and me. A great mentor is only as far away as your computer or the local library or bookshop. In this book I will share my most valued information and lessons learnt from actual experience as a mother in business.

I'm not saying this way with my short cuts will be easy, but it will certainly be no harder, and definitely much quicker. You will still need to take some action and work hard; but then you are already doing that, so why not take the short cuts and enjoy the ride.

Exclusive Limited FREE Offer
The Most Amazing FREE Gift Ever valued at $697

Yes! I can't wait to take you up on your amazing FREE offer where I get the complete CD & DVD set of Mal Emery and Madame Marketing's own marketing wisdom PLUS a selection of revealing interviews with the world's most incredible Millionaire Making entrepreneurs, including....

1. Breakthrough Marketing Strategies and Tactics PLUS 6 ADVANCED Marketing Secrets DVD.

2. The 7 Most Important Changes, Trends & Opportunities in Info Marketing Today Featuring Dan Kennedy.

3. The Ultimate Info-Marketing Shortcut: Bill Glazer's A-to-Z Info Business Blueprint for Info-Marketers.

4. "How to Master the Single Critical Skill that Pours Money into Your Bank Account, Day and Night... Almost like Magic" featuring Yanik Silver.

5. Mal Emery interviews Harry S. Dent, the author of "The Great Boom Ahead", about his predictions for the future of business and investing in stocks, shares and real estate.

6. Mal Emery interviews DC Cordova - DC reveals her and Robert Kiyosaki's Business Success Model - Masters, Niche, Leverage, Aligned Team, Synergy and Results.

7. Interview with Chris Payne: "The 4 Lies Your Mind Tells You Which Can Create Sadness, Frustration and Anxiety and Hold You Back From the Riches You Deserve."

8. Interview with Ted Nicholas: "World Renowned Author, Copywriter, Self-Publisher, Public Speaker and Direct Marketing Expert."

9. Interview with Paul Hartunian: "Professional Speaking on Your Feet" – famous for selling the Brooklyn Bridge.

10. Dr. Gene Landrum "Spills the beans on the Laws of Entrepreneurship that he has explored through the lives and achievements of 12 of the world's most eminent entrepreneurs."

11. Wonderful Web Women interviews Madame Marketing on how to create a "Mastermind Group" that get's results and ALSO reveals her negotiating strategies to get a better deal 9 out of 10 times, and NEVER PAY RETAIL AGAIN.

12.	Interview with Madame Marketing where she uncovers the 'BREAK-THROUGH MILLION DOLLAR PRODUCT" that generated her business over $1 million dollars and how you can adapt it to sell it in your business too.

PLUS you get to "Test Drive" for a full 3 months the "Madame Marketing's Closed Door Secrets" for members only, where she "pulls back the curtain on what actually works in Marketing with her exclusive on-line coaching programme. Email her any-time with your marketing challenges. See where she reveals the STUFF THAT WORKS! Have your own Marketing Coach as close as your computer, ready to give you the fast track secrets, or bounce ideas off. After a full 3 months FREE, unless directed otherwise we will continue to send you the "closed door marketing secrets" and give you access to Madame Marketing via email and charge your credit card $47.

Of course if you don't wish to continue to access "Madame Marketing's Closed Door Secrets" or have your own on-line Marketing Coach, simply tell us by phone on 1800 247 835 or email: info@madamemarketing.com and we will cancel your membership immediately and not charge your credit card another cent. No questions asked!

Please note you will be charged a one off postage and handling fee of $15.

Name:_____Date:_____

Address:_____

Suburb/State/Postcode:_____

Phone:_____Fax:_____Mobile:_____

Email Address:_____

Credit Card number: _ _ _ _ / _ _ _ _ / _ _ _ _ / _ _ _ _ Exp date _ _ / _ _

Signature: _____card 3-4 digit security code_____

Simply FAX THIS FORM TO AUSTRALIA:- 02 433 33493

GETTING 'ON TOP' SECRET NUMBER

1:

Find out what you are good at and systemise the rest!

Finding out what you are good at, then systemising and delegating the rest would be the ideal business world. It is what you can work towards. However, in reality it's important in business to understand your personal strengths and weaknesses first. The faster you do this the easier business life is. I'm not asking you to just find your "passion". I'm asking you to define who you are and what skills and attributes you have. You see I'm passionate about spending time with my kids, and going out to restaurants with friends. But I'm yet to have someone pay me for it!

What I'm talking about are things that flow freely for you in a business sense. What are the top 3 things you do in your business that really boost the bottom line? Are you good at organizing, selling, communicating, writing? Are you good with numbers, problem solving, negotiating?

Working out what you are good at and then focusing on it will give you the fastest and best results. The faster you focus on these skills, the faster you can break down what tasks it takes to run your business and what you should be doing in it. The faster you get yourself doing what you are most effective at and delegating to others what they are most effective at, the faster you will grow your business and start working on it, not in it.

Time to Systemise

Michael Gerber has written the most brilliant book on this, called The E-Myth. In a nutshell, the E-Myth is the Entrepreneurial Myth. The myth that business owners have to do it all, to be successful. It explains in detail how to systemize your business so you are not tied to it. If you are just starting in business, you may need to do everything at first. Your focus however should be on growing your business to leverage yourself out of it. You can't do it all and keep growing. You will need employees and systems for your business to grow. This also applies if you work from home.

This was a hard lesson for me to learn. I suppose at the time I thought that I could do it better and faster than anyone else, so why bother explaining it all. It took time to explain everything, and half the time I had to explain things more than once.

My biggest lesson was learning that 90% is ok. I was giving 110% in customer satisfaction, but really only 90% was required and expected. Expected is the key. My customers seemed happy with the service and quality my staff gave, just as much as the service I gave. In my eyes (for a time) I thought I could do better, but in reality my staff were more than competent to handle all situations that arose.

The secret to making this happen smoothly is systemising what you do. You have to systemise it so simply that anyone can do it. Systemising is going step by step through the processes of each task. I also like to put some trouble shooting suggestions in each system too. By that I mean, I like to write down what can go wrong, and what to look out for to ensure it doesn't. If something does go wrong, what to do to fix it.

We had been in business several years and were
working really long hours. We were involved in almost
every element of our business to make it work.
I felt I never saw the children and although
we were making great money I often joked I never
had time to spend any of it. I knew this wasn't my version
of what a successful mum in business was. We learnt
about systemising and knew we must do it, but again,
I couldn't work out how we could find the time.
It seemed like such an overwhelming task.
We decided to take a weekend off from the business
and go away to a bush retreat with our computer.
We sat there over 3 days and went through every
element of our business and wrote a system around it.
We wrote job descriptions for our staff and ourselves.
We wrote purchasing and ordering systems for our suppliers.
We wrote marketing systems for generating leads
for our business. All of this information was in our head,
it was just a matter of getting it out and on paper.
By the end of the weekend we had a complete manual
of how we like our business to run.

I remember once going to a seminar on "systemising". I had figured out the systemising part and done it. My next problem seemed to be to get the staff to follow the systems. They had been so use to me explaining everything verbally and being able to come to me to ask any question and solve any problem, that they resisted having to rely on the systems. The speaker told me that now I had written the systems my new job was to make sure they happened. Kind of like the professional nag! Rather than answer question after question, I would refer them to the manual. The other thing I would do was to ask them what they thought they should do, or ask them what the system was? When systems were not being followed, my new job became checking on them and gently reminding them to follow the procedures and reminding the staff that the systems were designed to make things easier for everyone. It didn't take long for our staff to take on more responsibility and for me to hang back a bit and let them find the solutions.

When I use the expression "employing staff" it could take the form of a bookkeeper, or even a cleaner to free up more of your productive time. You can still systemise these people in your life by giving them really clear directions on what tasks you expect them to complete and the time frame to complete it in.

This is how you can create the lifestyle. But be aware that if you are to grow a business to the point where you are not working in it all the time, you must give up some of the jobs. The jobs to get rid of first are the ones you are not good at or that you do not like. Other tasks to delegate first are tasks that can be done at a cheaper hourly rate than you would like to pay yourself.

I found I got a lot of clarity when I had a personality test done. There are some personality tests that relate particularly to business. It's also important to get your business or life partner to do one too. In my particular case, my husband and I have done personality tests to determine our own particular strengths and weaknesses. This is not so that in an argument we can point out each other's faults and shortcomings, but so we can fall back on each other's strengths to maximize any situation. Once you have worked out what you are good at, you then will also realize what you are not so good at. Don't despair. Sometimes your business partner, by some stroke of luck, is good at the things you aren't good at. If not, then you have a great opportunity to outsource or delegate.

A 10 minute personality test is available on
Madamemarketing.com.au
specially designed for people in business.

The next person I would hire, would be a finance person

I have some very successful friends in business, who have built up two successful businesses from scratch, the 2nd one to a 10 million dollar business. Many years ago I was going through some growth problems with our first business and was just not coping. They gave me some fantastic advice. Once they got the business going, they decided that the next person they would hire, would be someone to do the bookwork. They could then concentrate on managing the business and the growth of the sales. The first time around they made the mistake of getting more and more sales. Business floundered, things started to fall apart.

We had the same situation and my husband realised that

although he was good with numbers, he was not a trained Accountant. As things got bigger and more complicated, it became too much for him. Realising this and getting the right help before it was too late was a great step for us. This step could take the form of a great bookkeeper once a week or good accounting advice regularly. Another obstacle to managing growth of a business is not having systems in place to manage your sales. With one of our businesses we started by putting systems in place for purchasing and sales. We did this before we did any marketing or sales generating advertising. Just by putting systems in place increased the turnover by 15%. Creating systems around the sales and purchasing made everyone more efficient and the sales flowed easier.

The pocket rocket is next

The next person to consider hiring is your pocket rocket. These little gems are rare, but wonderful. A pocket rocket employee doesn't mind doing any job that needs to be done. They'll stay for however long they are needed to get the job done.

They look after the small details in an incredibly loyal way. They organize you and make you more productive. They start out doing the menial jobs, but eventually could run the place - if you wanted them to. They have a strong work ethic and love the job. These people do exist. They sometimes come in the form of secretaries or personal assistants. What I am trying to say is, when you hire the next person, make sure they have the right attitude and integrity. It is more important to find a person that fits within your culture than one with the most education.

When you do start getting some extra help, there is a saying in business, "Hire when you can half afford it". This means, if you can half afford their wage, and you are really busy doing it all yourself, then employ someone. The time they free up for you to work on your business will bring more money to you. I have worked this formula several times and it really does work. If you want to be cautious, start them part-time and see how they go.

Is your business that special?

Once you've worked yourself out, its time to look at the business. There is a business management practice - called the S.W.O.T analysis. S.W.O.T stands for Strengths, Weaknesses, Opportunities and Threats.

For the purpose of fast-tracking you to the top, lets examine the first one: Strengths. You must know what the strengths of your business are. You must understand why your customers choose you over the competitor. Please don't tell me it's your fantastic customer service! Everyone says that, even the big department stores, but have you ever tried to get any 'customer service' in one of them when you need it? What is it about your customer service that is so fantastic? Think about this for a minute, write down a list of all the great things you do for your customers.

Tell me the fantastic things you do that would make me shop with you? What is unique about you? What guarantees can you give me about your product or service? If nothing comes to mind instantly, sit with it for a while longer. Ask your customers when they buy from you.

Why do you deal with me? You might be surprised by the answer.

Once you have defined what your business is good at, its time to look at what gives you the most profit as well. This is a really important point. Business is not a hobby. You are doing it to make money. If you can find something you are good at and it makes you a great profit, then fantastic. If you are struggling to define your company's strengths, and your personal strengths within the company, alarm bells should be going off.

I come across a lot of business people that stay with a business and push it up hill. It doesn't mean that the business may not work; it just may not work with you in it. It may not work because of the location or there is just not enough of a market to sustain your business. This leads me to my next point.

A hungry crowd

If you want a faster way to get on top in business, here it is. Find customers that want a product or service and give it to them. Sorry, it's too simple isn't it? Well, that's it: find a hungry crowd. Find what your customers really want.

So many times business people come up with an idea that they think would be good and that they like. They may have experienced it personally and think "well I liked it, so everyone else will." They talk about grabbing market share. I'll let you in on a secret. Successful business people, do it the other way around. They find a hungry market. Find out what the customers want and give it to them. Find out what frustrates and annoys them. Find out what takes up their time and money. Find out what keeps them awake at night. Then solve "THAT" problem. That's the fastest way to make money.

If you see a new opportunity for your business, ask yourself this – "who would really want this?" Don't ask "how can I sell this to my customers?" If the market is there then that's a start.

It's actually the first step and it's the one that most people miss.

So if you want explosive, fast results. Here is the formula:

Do what you are good at in a business that focuses on its profitable strengths and sells to a hungry crowd.

GETTING ON TOP SECRET NUMBER
2:

Know what and when to delegate!

I remember when we first started employing staff, years ago, my sister-in-law, a long time public servant working for local council made a few suggestions. She suggested we give our staff job descriptions. I explained to her we were just a small business and we didn't do those sorts of things – job descriptions only worked for big business. How wrong was I?. I now know if you run your business like a professional business it will only prosper. It is just as important for my husband and I to know what our responsibilities are, as it is for the staff, no matter how big or small your business is.

I later discovered that measuring staff performance only made it easier in the long term. Having job descriptions for my staff meant they knew what was expected of them and I could assess how well they were doing their job. It also made it easier to advertise and train staff. Having my own job description meant I could work out which duties I wanted to delegate next. There is a key management rule that applies here. If you spend a larger percentage of your day working on the things that you are not only good at, but that give you the most profit you will get your best and FASTEST results.

There is always a person to suit every job!

When Louise came for the job, she was really keen. She was a single mum with two small children at school and she was desperate to find something that fitted into school hours. The cleaning of the roasting ovens was taking up a lot of time and I knew I was more effective working on getting more sales, but always seemed short of time to do it. Louise took on the task with enthusiasm and it freed me up to grow the business. She was later trained up to run functions and became our main wedding coordinator. When we moved into larger commercial premises, she ran the kitchen preparation as well as any commercially qualified cook. She had her own business card and was an integral part of the growth of our business.

A note on delegating. Delegating doesn't mean, "abdicating". You still need to check that work has been done to a standard. Rather than doing the task, your new job becomes checking that it has been done.

I urge you to accept 90% standard for work your staff complete (even 80%). If you are a perfectionist this will be hard. Unless you want to do everything yourself, you must accept that things will not always be your version of perfect when others are doing the task. There are many ways to be right. That is the new price you pay for not doing everything yourself.

"Yeah, but who's the boss?"

Even if there is a husband and wife team as the owners, there still must be only one boss.

In one of our first businesses we were interviewed by the local University regarding a study they were doing on husbands and wives working together (co entrepreneurs). One of the questions was "Who is the boss?" and we proudly exclaimed we both were. "Who do the staff think is the boss?" was the next question. "We don't know", was our answer. And we didn't.

The staff laughed at us when we asked them. Actually they fell about laughing. We now realise why and how important it is to have really clearly defined duties and leadership. We decided that I would become the Director. I am a little better at time management and fortunately, or unfortunately, I can and do make the hard decisions you need in business without losing too much sleep over it.

To put it bluntly I can fire people or tell a supplier to pull their socks up in a firm, but polite way. Jim on the other hand is a diplomat, which is incredibly useful in dealing with difficult people. He is also an attention to detail person and a problem solver, which is great for creating systems and finding solutions.

We developed a company structure based on our strengths in the business. Even if there are only two of you, you still need to do this. It has ensured there is no confusion about who is responsible for what tasks and the workload can be evened out. Our job descriptions stated these responsibilities.

Head of Finance

My husband has a better head for figures than I do. I have made a point to understand them more, but he can work things out in his head a lot quicker than me. It's his strength. Numbers don't rattle him easily. He's the best person for the job. He also has a lot more attention to detail than me. I go a million miles an hour and get a lot done. He is more exact and would prefer to get things done right the first time. I know if someone rings about an accounting issue or the staff want to talk about it, they must speak to him, not me.

My husband is responsible for all things finance. He reports on it to me, he is accountable and responsible for what happens in this department of our business. If there are problems, he must sort them out. I'm not embarrassed that he is better at this than me. It makes good business sense and it is a business decision.

Head of Marketing & Sales

I not only have a passion for marketing, I seem to be good at it. I read a lot about it and discuss it with other business people.

I understand the statistics and how to measure my advertising on all sorts of ideas. I have tried most marketing strategies over the years. I am also very clear about who our target market is and what return I want on any dollar I spend. I have a clear budget I work to. My husband and the staff know that if a sales representative calls to try and tell us about a marketing or sales opportunity, they can only speak to me. I report to my husband at our meetings on what I am doing. I am responsible and accountable for the sales of the

13

company. If the business is not meeting its sales budget, it is up to me to work out why and fix it.

Each role has a job description, so we understand exactly what we are responsible for and all our staff have job descriptions.

What tasks do I do?

If you are not sure of what tasks are involved in your business, here is a list of ideas that may prompt you. It is a great idea to sit down with a coffee and work out where you spend your time.

As you go through the list ask yourself these questions..........

- What task am I responsible for now?
- What task can be/is done by someone else?
- What is my hourly rate?
- What hourly rate will someone else do it for me?
- What extra turnover – if any, do I need to cover this expense?

TASK	ME	OTHER	WEEKLY TIME
ADMINISTRATION			
Goal Setting			
Business Plan			
Budgeting			
Writing Systems & Procedures			
Trouble Shooting Insurances			
ACCOUNTING			
Profit & Loss Budgets			
Cash Flow Forecast			
Accounts Payable			
Accounts Receivable			
End of Month Duties			
GST - Business Activity Statement			
Company Tax			
Other Taxes.			
Balance Credit cards			
Balance all accounts			
PAYROLL			

TASK	ME	OTHER	WEEKLY TIME
Wages/Salaries			
Payroll Tax			
Superannuating			
Workers Compensation			
Fringe Benefits Tax			
Annual Leave Records			
Sick Leave Records			
HUMAN RESOURCES			
Preparation to recruit (write ads)			
Read Resume			
Interview			
Employee training			
Performance reviews			
Team building			
OCCUPATIONAL HEALTH & SAFETY			
Policy Statement			
Risk Assessments/ Management			

TASK	ME	OTHER	WEEKLY TIME
First Aid			
Accident Reporting			
OPERATIONS			
Purchasing Stock			
Receiving Stock			
Construction or making product			
Dispatching of goods			
Stock control			
Vehicle Fleet Maintenance			
MACHINERY/ EQUIPMENT/TOOLS			
Purchasing			
Maintenance			
MARKETING			
Research & Development			
Marketing Plan			
Preparation of Material.			
Measuring Response.			
Distribution			

TASK	ME	OTHER	WEEKLY TIME
Design			
Meeting with representatives			
SALES			
Creating Leads			
Quotes			
Follow Up			
Closing Sales			
Staff Training			
HOME DUTIES			
Cleaning House			
Ironing/Dry Cleaning			
Preparing Meals			
Mowing Lawns			
Washing Dog			
Child Minding			
Pool Cleaning			
Car Cleaning			
Cooking			

This does not mean this person assigned to the task has to DO IT all.

They are just responsible for getting it done.

If I didn't have any staff, my life would be easier...

I hear this from many business owners. I believe my life is easier with my staff. Let me explain.

One of my mentors, Brad Sugars, said to me once "you get the staff you deserve." It annoyed me at the time, because I had always found it so hard to get good staff before that. I now constantly get comments from customers about how good my staff are. One guy even tried to offer one of my staff members a job, right there in front of me. Then I finally got it. I don't put up with the wrong people any more. I also make sure I have a job description with Key Performance Indicators of what I expect of them. I also have worked out the best way to write the ads for staff. The old way that doesn't work is to write about what you want as an employer. The way to get better staff is to write the ad selling the benefits of the job. Tell them the opportunities and the great things about it and being part of your company.

Then write the minimum job requirements. When I write ads for staff now, whether in be on-line or in the paper, I sell the benefits and opportunities of the job first. I also make sure my logo is in the ad and it is a display ad. I figure, if I'm going to pay for an ad in the paper, I want my industry to know we are expanding and what a great place it is to work.

I do everything I can do to get the interview right:

- I do a personality assessment in the interview to see if they will fit in with my team.
- I get the other staff who will be working with them to sit in on second interviews to make sure they feel they could work with them.
- I prepare questions that I feel will sort people out. Ques-

tions usually relating to past difficult experiences to see how they would handle them.

- I always check references, THIS IS A MUST.

Despite this, sometimes I still get duds. From permanent to casuals, I've had people lie, talk themselves up to be charming at the interview and then turn out to have some drug habit I didn't know about.

I have given up beating myself up for making the wrong choice. I speak to them once if the indicators are not good and then I let them go. There is nothing worse for the team environment than to let a bad egg drag down the rest of the team. I would prefer to work short staffed than have the wrong person in the job. Don't think you are ever so desperate as to put up with a bad employee. It makes the rest of your team suffer and can have long term negative consequences.

I have organised a free report on 'how to cut through lies and hire great staff for small business' from Toby Marshall at Abacus Recruitment.
Toby has over 27 years experience in the recruitment industry, but better still, he specialises in small business. He has some incredibly innovative ideas for finding and keeping great staff. Go to www.abacusrecruit.com.au/mmarketing

VALUED AT $27!

Once I realise I have a good employee, I look after them. I am very flexible with our staff regarding time off, family time and holidays. I am generous with gifts and incentives for a job well done and very generous with praise.

I often involve them with decision-making and give them a generous amount of responsibility. If they make a mistake, we discuss how it could be handled better and what would be a clearer way to go about it next time. We can all make mistakes and we all can learn from the experience.

One of my business mentors told me:

Look after your staff, they look after your customers, your customers will be happy and buy and they in turn look after your profits.

I still keep a line in the sand between boss and staff. It's often hard because some of our staff I really like as people, but if they do step out of line, I politely but firmly let them know. I often come home feeling lousy when I've had to reprimand one of them about something they have done, but there are jobs that have to be done, and it always works out better for the long term. My Dad used to say, "No one goes to work to fail". So often a gentle reminder to pull your socks up is all that is needed; however, this is one of the biggest problems my friends in business face.

Learning from mistakes

We once had one of our staff over-order a slow moving product. Instead of ordering 12, she ordered 122. She accidentally pushed the button twice on the computer and in her haste didn't pick in up. I noticed the excess stock in store and she tried to cover it up saying the supplier accidentally sent too many. I did a little investigating and found out what had happened.

I didn't make a big deal out of it, but asked if she needed more help and training in doing the ordering. She confessed to her error. We then worked out together how we could solve the problem. I explained in the early days I had made the same mistake, which I had. There was no yelling or reprimanding on my part, but she now knew that I was still aware of what happens in the day to day running of the business and now she was really clear that she needed to be more careful. She was also clear that she had my support that it is ok to make mistakes and that most problems can be fixed when they are out in the open.

It's easy to be nice to staff. But the courageous manager makes the hard decisions. When they are not working to the standards you require it is time to talk to them about it.

Whingeing and complaining about them to everyone else is a destructive way to manage people.

The problem gets worse and worse and then out of control. If you are really clear about what you expect of your staff a gentle reminder to bring them back into line is all that is needed.

Bad behaviour from employees starts off small. I'm not talking about when they have an accident or mess something up. I'm talking about continually being late, not following proper sales procedures, therefore not getting sales, and being rude or not speaking to customers or other staff correctly. This sort of behaviour needs to be jumped on straight away. Yes, you may feel lousy for a little while, but it is worth it. Even when it is not done on purpose it still needs to be talked about, but treat it as a learning opportunity. Perhaps a system can be developed and eliminate this situation in the future.

What if you train them and they leave?

We insist on training our staff. I love the quote by Tom O'Toole, when asked by a friend "what if you train your staff and they leave?", and his reply "what if I don't and they stay?"

One of the first things we do with permanent staff after they have been with us for a while is take them on a day out to check out the competition. They pretend to be customers and see what sort of service they get. They see how things are displayed and what items are featured. This seems to really pump them up and motivate them.

We also make sure they get correct training in sales, negotiation and conflict resolution. We have weekly meetings to discuss what is going on. My favourite is our monthly breakfast at one of our customers' businesses. Our customers love to see us in their café, and we enjoy it too.

How to fire staff

I can do this, but I don't enjoy it. Actually, who would? When you have the wrong person in your team, it is toxic. Toxic for you, toxic for your business and toxic for everyone around you. It is not a good wealth creation strategy.

Having the courage to get rid of a bad employee is diffi-cult, but it has to be done. Most of the time bad employees know when their time is coming to an end, and have usually started looking for another job - often in your time, and with your computer. I cannot stress enough; it is incredibly impor-tant to take control of the situation and get rid of this toxic person NOW. You are better off working under-staffed with a great team in synergy, than having a bad egg in the group.

Use phrases like "This is not working out is it...? Then let them be the next person to speak. Adding, "I think we should call it quits. How about I make up your final pay and you can go and do something that you will enjoy and is more what you are looking for?"

I recommend you don't take on other people's personal baggage and problems. I am not saying do not show com-passion. Often some wise words of advice and support from a caring person in authority is all that is needed. Sometimes some time off to sort personal issues out is useful. However, at the end of the day you have a business to run. Some em-ployees personal lives will spiral out of control whether you help them or not.

Sometimes it is better to let them go and sort themselves out, leaving the door open for a return when their lives get back together. I have, on occasion offered an extra week's pay and let them go straight away. Just to make the situa-tion easier.

Every businessperson I know feels lousy and emotionally drained when firing staff. The other feeling you get is relief. The benefit after the event is you get a good night's sleep.

"If I wake up three mornings in a row thinking about you and I'm not having sex with you, you've got to go" Dan Kennedy.

GETTING ON TOP SECRET NUMBER
3:

My perfect 3 - the perfect customer, the perfect product and a hungry crowd

Knowing this information will fast-track your results.

It is absolutely essential. Your perfect customer can be different for all businesses, but the bottom line is, your perfect customer is one who gives you a profitable sale - many times over.

Firstly, how do you get a profitable sale? You have to know what one looks like. You have to be really clear on what is profitable for you. There are a few ways to analyse this.

1) What is your most profitable product or service?

What product or service gives you your highest margins and/or higher dollar value?

This can now be a targeted product for your marketing. When you are aware which product or service is most profitable, you can give it more exposure. Put it at the front of your brochure. Display it at the front of your shop. Include it on the front of your website. Mention it at every opportunity. Once you are aware of it, give it all the attention it deserves. You can package it and market it to make it more appealing to your customers. By knowing what your most profitable product or service is, you will have an advantage when negotiating with suppliers. You will be able to negotiate bulk discounts because you will make it a popular purchase and therefore sell more of it.

2) Know your most profitable customer and target them

Let's now call them your "A" clients. Be really specific about who they are. What gender are they? What do they do? How much do they spend with you? How regularly do they spend with you? Do they recommend you? Do they spend more than the average customer? Do they purchase your high profit goods or services? Do they pay you regularly and without fuss? A valuable profitable customer would ideally do all of the above or a combination of most of the above.

If you own a café, your perfect customer might look like this.

- Buys a coffee everyday (that's a high profit product).
- Returns for lunch 3 days a week (regular customer).
- Works locally in business (easy to find and advertise to).
- Pays on the spot, without questioning price (cash up front, no haggling).
- Brings his/her friends in too (refers business).
- Brings clients in for meetings (spends more than average customer).
- Nice person to deal with (It's a nice day at work for me too).

This customer is buying regularly, often more than the average customer. They buy high profit products from you. They refer business to you and they pay up front. Can you see how this is an attractive customer for a café?

There would be many opportunities to market to this type

of customer. There would be many ways to find this type of customer in a cost effective way. I will explain how in my marketing secrets later.

Notice my last point, "a nice person to deal with". Write it in your criteria for your: 'perfect customer'. Life is too short to deal with jerks and customers who make you feel lousy. I have a business associate and she says daily **"I attract good money and good people"**. I have always instructed my staff not to put up with really rude people. It puts you in a bad mood for the rest of the day and makes you ineffective with the customers who really deserve your attention. All that is needed is a polite; "I don't think we will able to help you".

THE PERFECT CUSTOMER: I love the line in the movie "The People V's Larry Flint" about Larry Flint, the founder of the Hustler magazine in the US. He says to his attorney who didn't want Larry as a client any more; "Come on, I'm your perfect client, I've got lots of money and I'm always getting into trouble"

3) Now where do you find these perfect profitable customers?

A few questions you can ask yourself to find this answer are; who has them before you? Is there another business that does not compete with yours and has the same customers? Where do they live? What do they read or watch? Where do they search for your type of product or service? How do they like to shop with you - over the phone, in-store, Internet or via fax? Do they like to pay cash, credit card, or put it on account? Is there a list of your customers somewhere that you can get access to?

Are they part of an industry group or association that you can join or advertise with?.

You should be able to think of a couple of easy ways to find these people. This will be useful when you start targeting your marketing. This is the fast-track way to do marketing. So get really clear about where these people are and how you can find them.

If you don't know - FIND OUT! This is crucial to your marketing.

In small business we don't do mass media marketing. We don't have the budget! We do targeted specific measurable marketing. The most cost-effective way to market is straight to your target market. We have already discussed who they are and what is the most profitable service or product for them to buy. The next step is to find them. Obviously, the easier this is the better.

If you are having trouble, start collecting names of current customers. I'll explain later why this is so important. Make no mistake though; it is vital that you collect your customers' details and as much of their information as they will give to you.

To extract this information often requires some training. When you explain the benefits of you sending them special deals etc, they will be very happy to give you everything. Remember to tell them that their details remain confidential and are never given to anyone.

When the perfect customer calls your business or walks into your store, you know they are 'perfect'. When you design any advertising, you design it as if you were speaking directly to them and giving them what they want. If you want to purchase stock you know what will appeal to them because you already know what they want. It makes decisions about advertising and marketing so much easier.

Claim the position – be the expert

Once you've worked out who your perfect hungry customer is and what you and your company are good at, it's time to 'claim the position'. What I mean by this is, be the expert they go too. Be the perfect supplier to them. Let me explain.

The café I mentioned previously could claim its position as the 'Businesspersons' Café' The Café, local business people go to. The café to take clients to. The café to be seen at by the business community. Once you claim this position you then focus your marketing around making your business even more appealing to that specific clientele.

Claiming the position is about finding a niche within a niche. There could easily be five cafes in the same street, all doing a cake and coffee special. There could be six pest exterminators in the Yellow Pages, each killing all the bugs and creepy crawlies imaginable. There could be ten places on the web doing the same as you. It doesn't matter. This is the big secret in marketing:

Everyone else is trying to be "all things to all people".

That's the big lie in business and it doesn't work; yet 90% of businesses do it. If you take the time to be the expert and claim the position to the perfect customer, and then focus your marketing around them, you will find the shortcut to success.

I urge you not to worry about the business you are missing out on. It may seem like a big chunk of business, but really it's the scraps. It's the scrappy end of town that fights over low prices, low margins, rude people and slow payers. Follow my formula and you are following a formula that works.

I have seen it many times over. I see the coffee shop that puts in an ice-cream cabinet, because they noticed the guy down the road at the ice cream parlour seems to be busy. He thinks that must be the secret to business success - ice cream! Ice cream is not the secret. The guy down the road specializes in family deals. His ice cream shop is the place you go after your rushed dinner when the kids are going crazy and you need to leave the restaurant. You go to him to break up the meal. He gives free bibs to kids; a family discount and has high chairs with splash trays for toddlers.

I've seen the Indian restaurant owner introduce pizza, because the guy over the road at the Pizza restaurant is selling lots of pizza and he's heard its high profit margin. So pizza must be the answer. It's not. Pizza is not the answer. The reason the guy over the road is selling so much pizza is because he's defined his perfect customer and he's claimed the position.

He delivers 'bigger, better tasting pizza or your money back'. All his marketing is focused around giving his perfect customer what they want. That's why he's busy and making a load of money.

Keep in mind that 80% of your business will come from 20% of your customers. The fast-track way to making that work is to spend 80% of your marketing budget on that 20%.

My perfect customers

In one of my earlier businesses, a regional catering company, I sat down and worked out who were my perfect customers. I did a lot of 21st and 40th birthday celebrations, but weddings and corporate functions were usually my biggest dollar value and highly profitable. Weddings were more profitable because they often had three or more courses, as well as more guests and I was able to add on extra charges for drinks, staff and sub hiring of marquees, tables and chairs etc. Winning awards for these two target areas boosted my confidence to go after them and target them as my area of expertise.

I remember the first time I told one of my customers on the phone, "Weddings are our specialty. We do a lot of them and specialize in making it a perfect day for you." Later when she booked, she told me she had booked me because I specialized in weddings. Just claiming the position made me the local specialist.

I put together special packs for weddings, with menus ranging from budget to top of the range. I gave them brochures on recommended halls to hire, marquee hire companies and other related services I knew they needed and were of a high standard. Remember, if you recommend a bad business, your customer will link this business to you, so be selective. I added a page of testimonials of all the nice letters I had received from clients after their wedding thanking me. I presented it all in a beautiful white folder with my company details on it. They used to say they used that folder as their "wedding planning folder".

We later targeted our advertising to Wedding Magazines and joined Wedding supplier networking groups. Knowing whom our target market was, made it easier for us to decide where to spend our marketing money.

While weddings were always on a Saturday, my staff were not busy during the week.

Corporate Clients then became another target market I established. I always enjoyed being part of the local business community and often attended networking functions and business referral groups. It was such a nice way to do business in a friendly environment. I picked up many clients from networking, who later became friends. The business community is also very big on referrals, so it was a great way to get easy referrals for a job well done.

GETTING ON TOP SECRET NUMBER

4:

Know you breakeven!
Because...
"What gets measured is what gets done"

A friend of mine in business said to me recently," It always impresses me how you can rattle off what your break-even is, or your profit margins, or your customers average dollar, how do you know that stuff?" My answer could have been, "why don't YOU know that stuff?"

Your break-even point is that point in your business where your sales from your business cover all your costs. Once you know that you will be able to see exactly how many sales you need to make to get over the breakeven point and to start to make a profit. Don't forget to include the wage you would like to earn in your costings. Down the track if you decided to replace yourself or some of your duties, then you know the money is already there. I would also recommend you include any loan repayments for the business.

This way it is a true and accurate reflection of what the business needs to make to cover all its costs.

Not knowing your break even gives you a "false economy". You can see the money coming in because the cash register has more money in it at the end of the day; you know you are working hard, so you must be making money, right? WRONG.

Once you start measuring what you need to have, it's

amazing how money starts turning up. Knowing your break-even point leads to setting yourself some sales budgets. Having ways to measure your success and performance is just as important as it is for your staff. Your measurement indicators don't only have to be sales. They can be number of customers, number of units sold, average dollar of sale, margin of sale and conversion rate. You should measure all of them. If that seems too daunting, start small. But start measuring. Set yourself some goals to achieve and rewards to receive once they are accomplished.

Finding the break even

Early on in our business life, we were achieving great sales, working really long hours and not making any money. We thought it wasn't fair. Then our accountant asked us "Well what is your breakeven, what do you need to turnover every month just to cover your everyday costs and pay yourself a wage?" We didn't know.

When we sat down and worked it out, we found that although we were increasing our sales by 20% a month over the prior year, we needed a 30% increase, to cover our operating costs and pay ourselves a wage. After getting over the initial shock, we started to plan and work out how we could achieve it.

We reduced some of our overheads, changed phone companies and reduced our wages costs. We didn't actually reduce anyone's wages but we stream lined our operation so we didn't need staff the whole time. By staggering staff hours at functions we reduced our costs. Some staff started early and left early, others started late and left later. We became more efficient. We then set ourselves sales targets and budgets. Within 3 months we were regularly achieving over breakeven. We were actually making money! If you are not sure how to work out your breakeven your accountant will be able to help you. For an easy to use software spreadsheet to work it out yourself simply, go to www.madamemarketing.com.au

It is important to remember as your business grows and you leverage yourself out of the business, the breakeven will change. Each major change and extra cost you add to the business must be updated in your breakeven analysis.

Living within your means

"I've worked too long and too hard to eat sausages"

This was said to me by one of my friends, who would spend his last dollar on the latest gadget or holiday. He goes on more holidays than us, has twice as many televisions than us and eats out more than us. Don't get me wrong, we have a good life, but he is so in debt because of his life-style that he misses great opportunities.

Couples working together have to get this right. I know of people in business who are so out of sync on this one, it puts them backwards in life. When one of the couple spends more than they earn, it leaves the other feeling frustrated and resentful.

There seems to be an illusion that because you are in business, you should make an enormous amount of money and show the world how successful you are. Or the other theory seems to be that if you work hard, you deserve it, regardless of whether you are making money.

Remember if you keep buying "stuff", you'll finish with "stuff-all".

It feels so much more rewarding to buy yourself something special when you have budgeted for it and know you can afford it.

Working out a budget for home, life and investments can ease so much of the worry in business. After all arguments about money are the number one marriage killer! Think about school fees, sports fees, and insurance, right down to money you spend on gifts and take out meals. If you add it all up you can see where it goes.

Do the exercise, you'll be surprised where you can save money and where you could do things smarter.

HOUSEHOLD MONTHLY BUDGET

MONTHLY HOUSEHOLD INCOME		MONTHLY HOUSEHOLD EXPENSES	
Your Pay (after tax)	$	Rent or Mortgage	$
Partner's Pay (after tax)	$	Phone/Broadband	$
Investment Income	$	Electricity	$
Rental Income (after expenses)	$	Rates	$
Social Security Income	$	Vehicle (fuel, insurance, maintenance etc)	$
Child Support Income	$	Food/Alcohol	$
Other Income	$	Clothing	$
	$	Entertainment	$
	$	Fees/Interest (credit card, Vehicle, Charge Cards etc)	$
	$	Child Care	$
	$	Health Expenses (insurance premium & not covered by insurance	$
	$	Donations	$
	$	Gifts (Christmas, Anniversary, Birthdays etc)	$
	$	Personal Expenses	$
	$	Other Expenses	$
TOTAL	$	TOTAL	$

Budgeting for the future

There are so many books written on investments I won't go into this area. Invest in some of the books and seminars, and learn all you can. I will say that you need to put something away or have a plan to put something away regularly. When great investment opportunities present themselves you will be ready, cashed up and educated.

I see business as the key to building your wealth and cash-flow, but property and other investments are where you store it.

Educating yourself is the key. From my experience you are better off learning as much as you can about your own investments. That way you know a good deal when you see one. It also stops you from being misled. The statistics on poor, old people are staggering. Educate yourself, so you won't be one of them.

GETTING ON TOP SECRET NUMBER
5:

The 3 must have skills – Negotiating, Mathematics, Marketing

Learn to negotiate!

Make every deal a profitable one and only pay wholesale.

There will be many skills you will need and I would recommend that if you can't master them, delegate them. However, this is one that I insist you learn!

Firstly, negotiating is a skill you need for buying and selling and there are some fundamental elements to negotiating that are easy to pick up. I can easily account hundreds of thousands of dollars to my negotiating skills.

Negotiating to Buy

The basic principal you must think of when you make an offer in negotiating is 'what's in it for them'. There is a cheesy expression in marketing that says, tune into the right radio station. WIIFM. What's In It For Me. This is what the person you are negotiating in business is thinking.

Before you think about putting an offer together think of these principals:

- **What are their emotions around the situation?**

Who ever has the most emotions around the situation has the least power.

- **What is in the deal for them?**

Find out what they need or want, investigate and ask questions.

- **Is there a deadline?**

Whoever has the shorter deadline has less power.

- **What do I want out of the situation?**

Be really clear about what you want and always be prepared to walk away from the deal, if it doesn't work for you.

- **How can I make this win-win?**

Strive to make the deal work for both parties.

- **Be respectful to yourself and others.**

You will get a better deal if you don't back people into a corner or insult them.

If you are just asking for a better price there is one

golden rule. The one main phrase that will always help you when buying is "Is that your best price?"

That is all you have to say. You can use it from dress shops to used cars, to organizing printing for your business. There is usually at least another 10% in every deal, but if you don't ask, you'll never know.

Messed up negotiation

We were in between businesses and looking for something that would fit our criteria. I suppose I'd forgotten one of the golden rules with negotiating – be nice. I liked the business we were looking at – it had a huge up side, they were doing no marketing and were burnt out. It would have been an easy deal to do. Instead I told them what they were doing wrong with the business and the small amount I would offer them. They got their backs up and more or less told me to get lost. I don't blame them. I could have kicked myself when I realized what I had done. The next good deal that came along, I followed the formula. It saved me close to 40% of the asking price and better still everyone was happy.

There are a couple more elements to making it work. I treat it like a game. I might say, always smiling, "is that your best price? The game is, the next person to speak is the loser! Now 9 times out of 10, they will give you a better price. Sometimes they will justify the price and ramble on a bit. Just smile. They still may give you a discount.

Remember the old wives tale "you get more bees with honey," no need to be aggressive and rude. You will often get a better deal by being pleasant and charming.

Negotiating doesn't always have to be about getting a better price. I also like to use it for getting better terms. By terms, I mean the way I pay for the goods or services I am negotiating for. For example, consider some of the following when negotiating your terms:

- Payment terms extended. Ask for 60 days instead of 30 days.

- Payment can be split. Pay some this month, some next month or regular payments.

- Payment can be in the form of goods or services. Trading or bartering goods and services rather than cash can help everyone's cashflow. Be aware you still need to officially declare it to the tax department. However it is an option to help with cashflow.

The Win-Win Website.

We had a computer guy present us with a concept to take one of our businesses on line. He was very talented and creative and the price was reasonable. The only problem was we didn't have any excess cash lying around. Rather than borrow, we negotiated. I found out that he had a 4 day a week job and worked on his website building the other 3 days. He was passionate about designing websites. From that I established he wasn't relying on my money to pay his mortgage. I suggested paying the website off over 6 months. We started to pay before it was finished and doubling the repayments afterwards. The whole process was win-win. He was not out of pocket for his expenses, and we had a fabulous website that didn't stretch us financially.

The site paid for itself within 12 months.

If you feel embarrassed to ask, then get used to paying retail for everything. When I used to feel a bit self-conscious of asking I would think of the young teenagers at McDonalds who ask, "would you like fries with that"? How many rejections must they get before they get a sale, but they still do it?

Negotiation isn't always cash

We had been approached to do our first ever trade show. The brochure and marketing was slick and professional and they were the new kids on the block as far as trade shows went. I could see they were trying extra hard to compete in a competitive market and I really admired their style. The cost however seemed high, and I couldn't take a risk that the customers and sales would turn up at the show. So I made an offer. We negotiated the price to less than half the advertised price on two conditions. One that I would let my email customers know about the tradeshow. The other that I would supply cooking equipment for the demo kitchen at the trade show. This was a win-win cost effective negotiation for both of us. I emailed out to my clients and told them about the show. Many of them registered to attend. Then I contacted my suppliers and asked them to help me equip the demo kitchen, so the many famous celebrity chefs could use their equipment. They very generously supported the idea. The show was a huge success for the organisers, my suppliers and our company. Everybody benefited.

Negotiating to Sell.

When you are selling, it is just as important to be a good negotiator. This is where it helps if you already know your breakeven and your costing. I have trained all our staff in negotiating for buying and selling and I feel very confident with their skills.

If someone is buying a lot of goods, we happily give them a discount if they ask. If they are not buying a lot and ask anyway, we might suggest that they buy a carton or bulk items to get a discount.

Don't get me wrong; I'm not into heavy discounting or even discounting as a strategy to get more business. It's a fool's way to do business and the laziest way to sell. I do know however, what my margins are and my breakeven, so I know how much extra the customer needs to buy to make it worth my while. We also have a whole heap of useful free things we can give away for negotiating. If there is not much in the deal, we might say "Look that's the lowest I can go, but what if I throw in a couple of xyz for you and free delivery". We are already clear on the cost of the free goods, so we know what we are giving away. As I explain to our staff, most people just want a deal. Something for free is just as good. There are many ethnic groups who negotiate as part of their lifestyle. They just always ask for a discount. Being aware of this and not taking offence is a great strategy itself. Knowing they will be just as happy with getting something for free as a discount keeps everyone happy.

Sometimes they just need to know that they got a good deal. Often it is a cultural thing. When I have explained this to our staff they seem a lot more comfortable negotiating. They also see the playful side of negotiating and we often joke and laugh with our customers while we are working out a deal with them.

> ### *Everyone loves a freebie*
>
> *In our Catering days, we used to offer a platter of "free nibbles" as a negotiating incentive to choose our services over our competitors. The platter, we explained was something to snack on while the guests arrived and was often placed at the bar. We got many sales as a result of giving away "free nibbles. " The platter cost us about $30 and in those days the average function was around $1500.*

Learn basic business Mathematics

I know it can be boring; I used to find it that way too. I'm really not asking you to learn to do your own accountant's work. If you don't want to, don't. But you must learn what it all means. The basics you must learn:

-

- Break-even. You must know how much revenue (turnover in sales) it will take your business to do on a yearly, monthly, and weekly basis to cover all your fixed and variable costs. Make sure you include a wage for yourself. You then need to incorporate this amount in a budget for yourself.

- Budgets for sales forecasts and for spending. Set yourself a sales target with your newfound knowledge. I will discuss later how you can do the marketing to achieve it, but at this stage you must know what you are aiming for. You must also have a budget for your expenses. The main ones you should have are the cost of your goods as a percentage, and some of your major fixed costs like phone and electricity.

Knowing what you are paying out on your fixed costs per month helps you negotiate better contracts. If you can go to a phone company or a courier company and say "I'm spending $1000 a month, what's the best price you can do for me" you'll get a better deal. Look up madamemarketing.com.au for a template on how to set sales budgets.

- Cash flow versus Profit. Just because there are cheques left in the books, doesn't mean there is money in the account! Be aware of money coming into the business as well as money going out.

- Creditors versus Debtors Cycle. This is the length of time you have the money in your bank account. For example if you buy on a 30 day account from your suppliers, and sell on a 30-day account to your customers. The way to influence this is to make sure you keep on top of your customers who are on account. You also need to pay your suppliers as close to the due date as possible. Having a good relationship with them is just as important. I've had businesses where I got paid up front, before I had to pay for the goods and vice versa.

Either way, you need to keep on top of this. If you don't like following up debtors – delegate it out to someone else. It has to be done.

- Return on Your Investment. I use this formula for all sorts of things, but the main one I want to point out to you is for costing marketing and advertising spending. I suggest you always work out what it is costing you, and estimate what return you will get on the investment.

Write it down and it happens faster.

This formula works for goals, but it also works for setting sales targets and business budgets. How this universal law works is by writing down what you want to achieve, you seem to start finding ways and opportunities to make it happen. This was never more evident for me, than when we worked out our breakeven. As I mentioned earlier, we were doing great sales over the prior year, but it wasn't enough to cover our breakeven costs. Let alone make a profit. When we found out what we needed to do to break-even, and then on top of that make a profit, it seemed unbelievable. I look back now and think what a small amount we were aiming for. But at the time, we needed tens of thousands of extra dollars in sales.

We set the new sales targets, thinking in our hearts it seemed impossible. We were always looking for ways to get the extra sales and the more we looked the more we found and the more people we met who helped us learn. Within 3 months we were hitting our new target. That is the other universal. The 90 day rule. Once you become really clear what you are aiming for and focus on it with all your attention, you will almost always see a result within 90 days. Start some powerful action towards the goal you really want and believe in it. Plant seeds and be open for opportunities everywhere. Sow seeds, sow opportunity, talk to as many people and find as much information that you can. Massive action will get you massive results. Each and every time I have applied this principal, it has worked.

Setting the Targets.

For all the reasons above, it is important you have a sales target and a business budget. Tips to consider when you are setting your Sales Target are:

- What is your breakeven target?
- How much money do you want to make over 1 year. Then break it down to monthly goals?
- How much revenue do you need to make the money you want each month?
- Then start planning your marketing around how to make that happen?

Setting the Business Budget.

You also need to have some clear guidelines around what you will budget for the year in regards to your costs. This is where your costs can blow out and your breakeven can blowout if you are not monitoring your fixed costs. It also helps when you can estimate your variable costs, so you know your revenue will cover it all.

People say, "I need a good accountant." Well what is a good accountant? Your accountant is part of your team, like a sub-contractor to your business. You must give them as much instruction as possible regarding what you want done. I have involved our accountant in the process of working the aforementioned details out, but not all accountants will have the facilities or time to do that.

A mentor who is successful financially in business would also be a good person to talk to.

Need some help on this one?
Go to madamemarketing.com.au for our easy to use,
step by step breakeven spreadsheet. Which includes
a free copy of what to put in your business
and sales budget.

Learn basic marketing and sales

"The quality of your marketing will determine the ease of your sale" Mal Emery.

Picture this. Customers walking in your doors wanting what you have. No haggling, just handing over the money and happily walking off. Imagine the phone ringing with orders for you, customers with their credit card details, wanting to buy, they have already made the decision. No need to talk them into it, no need to offer a discount, no pushy sales talk, no cold calling. Imagine turning on your computer and paid orders sitting there waiting for you while you were sleeping.

Wouldn't it be easy? It's a dream right! No. This is what can happen with good marketing. Marketing is just a formula you can learn. Let me teach you some of the fast-track secrets.

Mathematics versus marketing

Make no mistakes - marketing is where the big dollars are. This is how you make money faster, when you get this right. In my opinion, you can still make money by just doing lots of cost cutting and getting your finances right, but it will be slow, and eventually you will start going backwards.

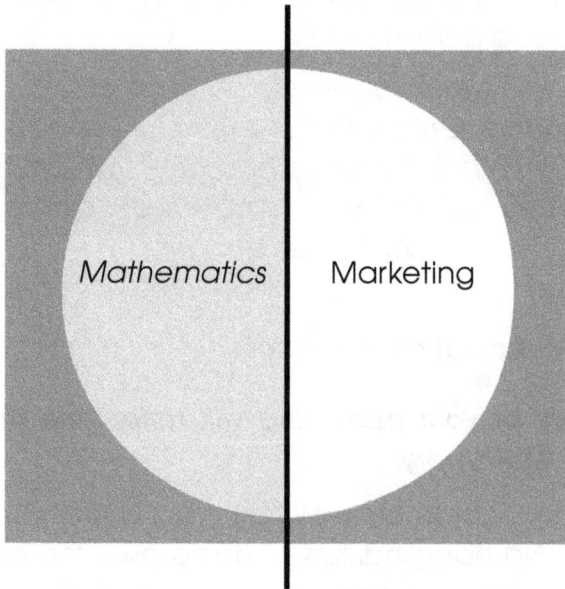

Marketing will fast-track your success.

A warning, if you don't get your finances right first, then sort out systems in your business, marketing will help you go broke faster. I love the expression,

REVENUE IS VANITY, PROFIT IS SANITY!

Marketing trickery

I was recently out at one of our favourite restaurants with some overseas relatives to celebrate a special family occasion. I recommended a particular bottle of wine that I really liked and proceeded to tell the story behind the name. "10 minutes by tractor" was the name of the wine. The story goes that this little boutique and exclusive vineyard was 10 minutes by tractor from the homestead.

The bottle has little faded tractor prints on it, and a cute picture of a tractor on the lid. The overseas visitors loved the story. Then one of my relatives commented, "just sounds like marketing trickery to me." From a marketing point of view, it was a beautiful bottle of wine, a lovely story to talk about over dinner, a memorable name and presentation that made it desirable to pick up. I couldn't see any trickery! We had another 2 bottles!

Marketing by my definition is giving the customer what they want, but I like to put an additional clause on that statement:

"Giving the customer what they want in the most profitable way for me"

Isn't everyone happy then? The customer has what they want and I have a profitable business. There is no trickery and there doesn't have to be. There are however formulas; easy to follow formulas. Let me explain.

Now the skeptics are already saying. "That won't work, my customers just want the cheapest they can get and that's not profitable for me". I used to think like that too. It's wrong. If customers were only driven by price, then people wouldn't buy Mercedes or designer clothes or jewellery. And besides, what is cheap? I know for a fact, some of those huge discount type shops still make 100% mark-up. How do I know? I've bought and sold similar products, at 100% mark-up. That is profit plus giving the customer a cheap price, isn't it? Don't assume it can't be done. Find a way to make it happen.

Before we can launch into the formula, you should have already worked out:

- What your breakeven is?
- What Sales you need to give you the income you want.
- What you are personally good at?
- What your business is good at & most profitable at?
- Who is your perfect customer?

A word on sales

We are always selling. We are selling by the way we dress, by the way we present our goods and services and how we speak to our customers. Getting your marketing right will make your sales easier. If you really are uncomfortable with sales, get really good at marketing.

If I could give you one key point to remember about sales, it's TRUST. You must earn your customers trust. When I hear people say that "she's got a bubbly personality, she'd be good at sales", it shows me how little they know about sales. Personality is half the story. To me, it is not even the main point.

The person who is good at sales is the one who LISTENS and who the customer trusts. Sales are a learned skill. You don't have to have a bubbly personality to be good at sales. It certainly helps to have a pleasant nature, but you don't have to be over the top. I've had sales representatives walk into my business, and you'd swear they had 6 cups of coffee before they walked in. I've had them talking at me at a million miles an hour, in an hysterical tone. On the flipside, I've had sales representatives walk into my business, tired and exhausted and begin to tell me their problems. Not only do they tell me their problems, they tell me how bad business is. I'm not really interested. As we all know, we have enough problems in business ourselves, we don't need to hear anymore.

You don't need to be a master of trickery and manipulation to be good at sales. I have had sales people work for me who are very serious, conservative, people and they are very successful. They are successful because they listen to the customer, they ask questions and they never ever let their customer down. The customer trusts them. The important things to remember in sales are:

- It's not about you. It's about them. Make the conversation about them.
- Listen. Listen. Listen.
- Build rapport and trust. Find common ground and find their interests.
- Solve their problems with your products or service.
- Deliver what you promise.

The skills you need to learn are the signals your customers give you. You need to learn buying signals. You need to learn signals on when to ask for the sale. You need to learn signals on when to ask more questions. These are all learned behaviour and they are easy to follow formulas.

When I question my friends in business who feel they are not good at sales, I have found that their biggest obstacle is a fear of rejection. You can dramatically reduce your rejection rate by being really clear about what your customer wants. Then you have to present it to them in a way they want to buy it.

I have personally interviewed a successful woman in sales to explain the shortcuts to sales success. She addresses how to build rapport, how to recognize the buying triggers, and how to ask for the sale. She also reveals some of the secret advantages that women have in sales over men, and it's not what you think! Check out the link at madamemarketing. com.au

A word on rejection

If you are in business, you will have to get used to a bit of rejection. I love the line "what someone thinks of me is none of my business". My other favourite is "great spirits will always encounter violent opposition from mediocre minds". It helps for me to imagine that the person who is being rude to me is having a bad day and I just happened to walk into the situation at the wrong time. I often think to myself, they will be racked with guilt for being so mean. In reality, they probably won't, but it helps me, so who cares.

Touch me five times and I'll buy

There is a theory in sales that is takes five "touches" to get a sale from a cold call. Basically, if they have never heard of you before, they may need to see you or you may need to be in front of them "five times" until they have enough trust in you to buy from you.

If marketing is supporting your company to make sales easier, than "touching" your perfect customer and being in front of them through different marketing channels will make the message clearer. That is why my concept of the marketing chair is so important. I have always tried to use different media to get my customers attention. It would be arrogant to assume that your customer is ready to buy off you the exact day you decide to send them an email or direct mail piece. You have to be constantly funnelling different opportunities to them to get them at just the right time. With over 40,000 marketing messages in front of most people everyday, it is important to remember a 'perfect hit' on the 'perfect day' to the perfect person' is just a numbers game. You elevate the numbers by hitting them at different angles and with different media.

Madame Marketing's 'getting on top tip' for marketing:

The cheapest, fastest, most cost effective thing you'll ever do!

This one simple function in your business will fast-track your marketing. It will save you money and make your marketing so much more cost effective. This is a fasttrack secret you must do.

A good, clean database is one of the most valuable marketing assets you can have. If you want your marketing to be cost effective, start developing your database as early as possible even if you don't use it straight away. File the details somewhere. It will save you so much time and money on your advertising and marketing down the track.

You should be collecting your clients' name, address, phone, mobile phone, fax and email address as soon as possible. Later you can get birthdays and special occasions, their purchasing patterns, likes and dislikes. My current database is worth thousands of dollars. How do I know that?

I have been offered thousands of dollars to promote other companies products and services on it. It is clean, targeted and the clients on it are warm and friendly to me. They trust me.

The fastest way to collect your database

The website was planned to go live in late April. I started planning the marketing before hand. We already had a strong database of customers' addresses, so I would definitely let them know about our new website, but I needed email addresses fast.

I organised an incentive in store for our staff to collect as many email addresses as they could from our customers. I would pay them 50 cents per email address, with a bonus for whoever got the most addresses. It became a game for them. This quickly added up to hundreds of dollars and I had a readymade list of my target audience. They were permission based and liked us already. On our first live day of our website we sent an email out to our newly created email database and got an order within 24 hours. The web designer had never seen an instant response like it.

One of the fastest ways to grow your business is to share your database with other like-minded companies, Companies that may have similar targeted customers, but not similar products. This is called a business joint venture. What I mean is you recommend their products to your database and they recommend you to their database.

There have been studies done on this in the United States. They compared companies in the United States who shared their databases with companies in Europe who would not share. The United States companies grew at an incredibly faster rate than their European competitors.

Remember advertising is an investment, not an expense!

There is a joke in advertising that "only 50% of advertising works, but nobody knows which 50%".

Let me explain that advertising is an element of marketing. You can market your business without advertising. An example is networking - networking is marketing your business. However you must understand that when it comes to spending money on your business by advertising, it is an investment. You want a return on it. You are not doing it for fun or to look good or to impress people. When you spend money on advertising in your business, you should have an idea of what you will expect in return.

I am known for targeted, measurable marketing. I only do marketing that I can measure. Some advertising reps love me for it; others hate me, because they can't justify how their advertising works. By measurable marketing, that means I always have a call to action, an offer on my marketing. If not, I have some way I can relate the sales generated from the advertising or promotion back to the money I spend. Because I do that, I estimate what return I should expect from my investment.

It took me a while to work out exactly what to measure. I had read all the books and heard the seminars about 'testing and measuring' your marketing. The trouble was, I couldn't work out what to test and measure! What indicators did I need to be looking for? I have since found out there are industry standards of what responses to expect. By knowing what the industry standards are for each form of media, you can help calculate what you think you should get back before you start spending money. There are also ways to manipulate these figures and get explosive results.

The types of ideas that get explosive results can sometimes cost more money, so you have to be really clear on what your profit margins are and what you expect to get in return. If you are not sure what sort of results to expect, ask your local advertising representative. I have a list of industry standards for advertising on my website madamemarketing.com.au.

Just because you spend loads of money, doesn't mean you will get a fantastic return. I am usually conservative. I work on never spending more than 5% of turnover. This figure is irrelevant as it depends on what your profit and margins are. I just find it works for me at this moment. The figure will vary depending on what your profit is, and how much "lifetime value" a customer is worth to you. So I suggest you create a budget that you are comfortable with and stick to it. If you feel as though you are spending money on advertising and it is hard to measure or it doesn't work. STOP IT NOW.

Competing with the Jones'....

I still help out with marketing for one of the people that bought a former business of ours. One day she rang me in a panic because she had been told a new competitor on the scene was taking out a full page Yellow Pages Ad and she had only booked a half page.

It wasn't too late to change it and invest almost $20,000 in the ad. I calmly explained that I knew and she knew that the business couldn't afford to spend $20,000 alone on that one ad. There wasn't enough return in it. Besides if people go to the Yellow Pages they usually ring more than one company. I explained she would win out on her other marketing and customer service. She took my advice and, sure enough, when the Yellow Pages came out, the new hot shot on the scene had taken the bigger ad.

She was frantic with worry. I kept saying he can't afford it, he can't afford it. You have over 10 years reputation and a great customer database; he is starting from scratch and paying big dollars on one form of advertising. It will not generate enough money for him. He was closed within the year.

No offer = No action

I was mentoring a group of women new to business and had a question and answer section at the end of my presentation. One of the women asked me "How do I follow up the people that I've dropped leaflets to in their letterbox?" I found out she had dropped a leaflet into the letterbox of local business people, who were her target market. Fantastic. I explained it was hard to follow up that way and asked what the offer was on the leaflet? "I didn't give them an offer; I just gave them my phone number and told them what I do." She replied. "Why would they call you?" I asked. No one had phoned her. She was doing it the hard way. One of the ways you can test your marketing is to test the offer you use. Some offers will work better than others. I will explain later what works better. Just know that there must be an offer or 'a call to action'. You must give them a reason to act.

When I am putting together an advertising campaign I cost it out beforehand. This is so I am not going into it blindly. It is also a useful tool when things work really well.

I have already costed it out, with the return I usually get. I test and measure it until I find a winning formula. Then I stick to it. This is when you can start going to your suppliers with actual results and ask them to contribute. It's a safe investment for them and it reduces my costs even further.

The marketing costing analyser

With the profitable marketing magic, you firstly write down how much a certain project will cost you. For example if you were looking at a direct mail campaign you may take into account printing, artwork and distribution. If you have one of your suppliers or business joint venture partners contributing to the promotion, you deduct that off the cost. I will explain how to get them to contribute later.

Once you have worked out your cost. You work out how much revenue (turnover) you need to cover this cost. You do this by working out the average margin you make. This will give you an idea of what you need to turnover to pay for this promotion.

You can now see if this is a feasible advertising or marketing campaign. To breakdown whether it is feasible or not you need to look at the increase in sales of the products or services you are offering. If you go onto the madamemarketing.com.au website this process is automated. You can just put in costings and margins and it will work it out for you. Alternatively, you can use the worksheets provided below.

PROFITABLE MARKETING MAGIC			
Costing Description	Quantities	Cost	Supplier
ARTWORK			
PRINTING			
DISTRIBUTION DIRECT MAIL (Include Postage)			
EMAIL OUT			
ADVERTISING PRINT MEDIA			
ADVERTISING TELEVISION			
ADVERTISING RADIO			
INSERT IN MAGAZINE/TRADE JOURNAL			
PUBLICITY			
SMS TEXT MESSAGING			
JV PARTNERSHIP			
FAX STREAM			
GIVE AWAY ITEMS/STOCK			
HIRE COSTS			
SUB TOTAL			
Less subsidy by supplier			
TOTAL COST OF MARKETING			
What is your average Gross Profit Cost as a percentage?			
Breakeven is Total Marketing Cost divided by Gross Profit %			
E.g.: $10,000 divided by 40% = $25,000 needed to breakeven			
SALES REQUIRED TO BREAKEVEN =			

Then write down the products and services you are featuring and measure their activity.

PRODUCT	CODE	COST	SELL	PROFIT	NO.OF SALES	PROFIT X SALES	REVENUE
TOTAL RETURN ON INVESTMENT							

Supplier contribution

You will find most of your suppliers will have budgets for advertising. I have found the most successful way to get suppliers to contribute to your advertising campaign is to make it a profitable venture for them.

Getting your supplier to pay for your Marketing is about honing your negotiating skills for a win–win situation. Your supplier is not a charity; they will want something in return. You should think of your suppliers as part of your team. They are there to help you be the best you can be. It is your job to convince your supplier that investing in your promotion or marketing concept will be financially beneficial to them.

Your Power Cards.

Knowing what you have that will impress them and persuade them will help a long way in the negotiations. As in a game of poker, you have to know what is important to them. You have to know what power you are holding to influence them.

Some key power cards are:

- How large your database is that you are targeting?
- How targeted your database is. Is it relevant to their product?
- How loyal are you to their product?
- Will there be any competition against their product?
- What guaranteed or estimated sales can you give them? Now or in the future?

The Good Idea.

The local Chairperson of the Restaurant and Catering Association asked me to sponsor a "Dessert Competition" amongst local Restaurants and Cafes. It was to promote the local hospitality industry, and advertising would be sent out to hundreds of local restaurants and cafes in the area. Our company would be promoted in the lead up to the event and on the day. We agreed to the sponsorship and gave extra prizes. We had local chefs coming into the store buying things to make their special desserts. We had terrific exposure on the day and made some great new customers and contacts. We also ate a lot of dessert!

The Bad Idea:

I once had a women come into our store and wanted me to sponsor her and pay for all her cooking equipment. I asked what the promotion was. She was going to start to do healthy cooking lessons to retirement villages. Although this seems like a lovely idea, there is no benefit to me as a supplier. She did not have an established base of customers. She was targeting retirement village residents, who are not my target market. She could not guarantee any of them would buy from our company later.

How can they help pay for the Marketing?

Payment does not always have to take the form of cash. Here are some examples of how your supplier could help with the cost of your Marketing:

- They could give you a credit on future stock.
- They could give you stock as free give always.
- They could give you stock instead of money.

- They could give you heavily discounted stock for the actual promotion.

- They could extend your payment terms for another 30 days to help with your cashflow.

- They could supply you with the promotion material you need. They often have access to cheaper printers or have already mass printed brochures with what you need.

- They could split your payment terms. Deliver everything you need for the promotion this month. Then only charge you for half of it this month, and half next month.

- They could give you a bulk discount on a certain items. Make sure you agree on the minimum number you have to buy up front. Also agree on any top up amounts. For example you agree to buy 10 at the discounted price, and if you sell more than 10 you buy every extra one at the buy in bulk price.

- They could pay for your brochure, or selected pages in your brochure on the condition that you only feature their products.

Prove yourself first....

I had only been in the business a little while, but I had done all my costing and I knew what I needed to make my promotion work. I needed a good deal on some cooking equipment to sell. My favourite supplier told me they didn't do that sort of thing. I showed them how I had planned the promotion out, and what I projected the sales to be. They still would not budge. We finally negotiated on an upfront order from me to them, heavily discounted, but with extended payment terms. I had to prove myself. The promotion was a huge success. We ordered another 3 times what the initially ' forced' order was. These days they ask me if they can go in the next promotion I do.

Build your marketing chair

I refer to my marketing strategy as my marketing chair. The great thing about a marketing chair, it doesn't have to cost a lot of money. What is important is that you have multiple channels of marketing in your business.

If you look at the top of the chair, you will realise, if you only had one leg, or for that matter one source of marketing coming into your business, the chair (the business) would fall over. The other problem with only having one source of marketing coming into your business is that is leaves you vulnerable. If that medium changes dramatically or a competitor masters it better than you, you have lost all your marketing in one foul swoop. The government can also change laws regarding advertising very fast. Make no mistake, relying on only one form of marketing or having all your 'eggs in one basket ' is one of the most dangerous things you can do in business. It is as dangerous as relying on only one customer.

I am often asked about email marketing and the website as cost effective marketing. On paper, email marketing would have to be the best return on your investment. However I can also tell you there is as much business off-line as on-line. What I mean by that is, people may get the email or look up your website, but they may still want to talk to a "real" person or visit a "real" store. Don't leave money on the table because you haven't considered other cost-effective ways to reach your perfect customer.

I have had businesses where I have over 14 different channels of marketing coming into it and generating sales and leads. Some of them costing thousands and others costing very little. All of them are measurable.

Legs on your chair could include:

- Yellow Pages
- Direct mail
- Lumpy mail
- Advertising in Press
- Inserts in trade publication
- Barter Exchange (Bartercard)
- Business card,
- Brochures
- Networking
- Sponsorship

- Website
- Emails
- Web optimiser
- Sales repping
- In-store promos
- Fax stream
- SMS messaging
- Charity
- Freebies

THE MARKETING CHAIR:

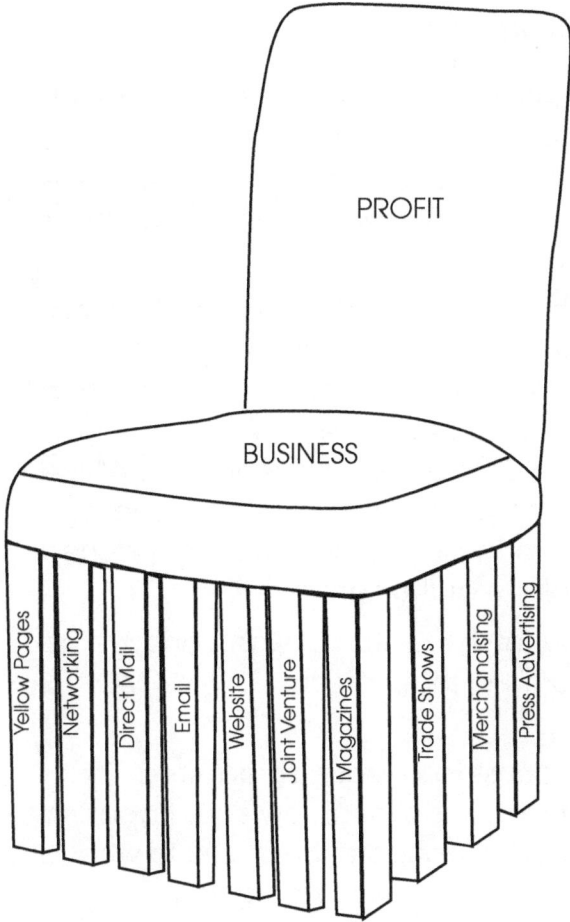

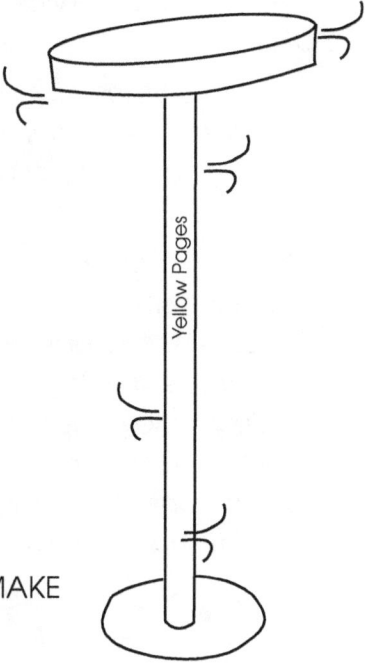

PROFIT

BUSINESS

Yellow Pages · Networking · Direct Mail · Email · Website · Joint Venture · Magazines · Trade Shows · Merchandising · Press Advertising

Yellow Pages

ONE FORM OF MARKETING CAN MAKE BUSINESS UNSTABLE

My favourite "P" for a hungry crowd

If you ever study marketing at tertiary level they will teach you the 4 "P's of marketing: Place, Price, Promotion, and Product. The basic theory is that by working on all of these elements of your business, you will master marketing. This is true - it's the long way, but it will work.

I have an extra "P" that I like to add. It's called "Perception". The short-cut way to mastering marketing is "Perception". It is back to finding what your customer wants and satisfying all their needs in a profitable way for you. How many times have we paid for something regardless of the price, because it was just the right colour, it was a package deal and we had to have the lot, or the special happened to appear at the right place at the right time?

If you do not find out what the customer wants and create the product or service around that, you are LEAVING MONEY ON THE TABLE.

So many times I hear people talk about a great idea. That's the slow track; it may work, but is a long, slow slog. If you find your self saying "I just need to educate the public to what a great idea this is" warning sirens should start going off.

The fast-track way is to find hungry customers, which really want something and then sell it to them. If you already have customers, find out what they want. Price it in a way that they perceive it is good value. Present it in a way that they perceive they need it NOW. Promote it in a way to ensure they will hear about it when they are ready to buy. Place it right in front of the hungry crowd, ready to spend. Make no mistake, that's the way to make money fast with marketing.

The sexiest word in marketing starts with "F"

It's FREE. Buy one get one free. Buy this product and get this product free. Ring me for a free report. FREE FREE FREE.

We love free. Free will always do better in a marketing promotion than a percentage off. Always. If you are going to run a marketing promotion and you are going to give a percentage off, don't even bother with anything less than 10%. 5% is an insult to your customers. And frankly, who is going to get out of bed for an extra 5%. It's not sexy.

FREE is sexy. Even rich people like free. Women loooovve free. Men like free too. Kids love free. FREE is popular.

When I talk about not getting out of bed for anything less than a great deal, I like to remind myself of the supermodels. There was a supermodel who declared she wouldn't get out of bed for anything less than $10,000 a day! You have to think of the offer you give people and ask yourself 'is it sexy enough? Would my perfect customer get out of bed and pick up the phone or run to my business for this offer?

Now I want to deliberately mention the marketing costing analyser before I started ranting on about sexy free stuff. You see, I didn't say give everything away and be the most popular poor businessperson in town.

You will be popular when you start giving stuff away, but let's make money too. Do not give anything away, until you have costed out the promotion. Free stuff is also about perception. What can you give away in your business, for FREE, that has perceived value of loads more than it cost you in time or money. There are a number of things you can give away for free, it doesn't just have to be product. Here are some examples I have personally used, or business people I know have used, which work really well.

FREE INFORMATION: Information is a great freebie. Giving away free information about your product or services also helps position you. Remember we need to be known as the local expert and claim the position.

I have a client who gives away a "free report" on how to get the best valuation on your house. She sells home loans. What type of people want to get their house valued? People who are thinking about getting a home loan. Does she know what you need to do to get the best valuation on your home? Yes. Does it cost her anything? Maybe a little time to write the report, but she only writes it once.

Would she get any qualified leads out of the people ringing for the free report? Yes, loads!

FREE PRODUCTS: This is where your suppliers can come in. I have a hairdressing client who gives away a free styling product with every fifth haircut. Its value is $19.95. Great Freebie. Her customers love it. She goes to her supplier and negotiates a deal to get the product in bulk and save 30%. It ends up costing her $5 each giveaway. The average haircut is $60. That's $300 worth of sales for a $5 gift. Is that good value for the customer? Yes. Is it a cost effective promotion for the hairdresser? Yes.

FREE TIME: This one I'm not so fussed about. It's open to abuse and limited. There are only 24 hours in any day. Once you get busy, you don't have any more time to give. It can work as an introduction to a service, but you have to be pretty confident in your sales ability to get a sale at the end and convince your client it's time to pay. It can only work, if done correctly.

The truth about brand advertising

Branding advertising versus cutting through the clutter

In my early days of business, I would discuss with a representative from the paper why my advert hadn't worked. They would always use the expression, "well at least if was good brand advertising." Argh!!!

In small business we don't do brand advertising or not like that anyway. We don't have the budgets of McDonalds or Coca Cola, so we have to do our branding or portray our image differently.

We do it by the way we present our business, by the way we dress, how we display our goods. It could be what our furniture is like, our cleanliness, staff uniforms, the car we drive, lighting, music, ambience, our business card and our logo. It's showing our customer what is unique about us. It's having a 30 second spiel about what you do, not leaving the person still puzzled about exactly what business you are in.

It's helping your customers cut through the clutter, so they can see you first.

What sort of image or feeling are you hoping to create? Your branding should fit with the image you hope to portray. Your brand or image is stronger when you become more specific about what it is you do. Think of the fantastic Irish Pubs. From the outside in, they create a feeling of fun, warmth and casual good times. What image do you want your business to portray? Making some adjustments to create the right image in your business can give the right perception to the customer. Branding is all about the little details.

A call to action

So how do we portray all of that in our advertising?

Firstly be aware of what image you want to portray. Then be aware of who you are wanting to impress. Be aware of your "Perfect Customer." Then ALWAYS, ALWAYS, have a call to ACTION. Give them a reason to contact you. Give them a reason to pick up the phone, place their order on line, come in and see you NOW.

A free offer, a great deal, a limited edition.

Work out what appeals to your customer and present it in such a way that they perceive that it's good value and you are trust worthy to do business with. Cut through the clutter by choosing advertising mediums that you know they will be watching, reading or seeing. Put the offer right in front of their face. When it works, measure it. Then do it again.

Marketing trickery exposed

I hesitate to write this, because personally I don't think its trickery. If you do, you need to realign your values around marketing. I see so many tremendously talented people who cannot communicate their greatness to their target market, but it never seems to be their fault. They see others, less talented than them who have mastered the art of "marketing trickery" reap the benefits of success and fortune.

That's the first rule in marketing trickery. It is not the smartest or most talented person who finishes first.

It's the best Marketer.

These talented and creative people respond by learning more and more about their area of expertise. At the same time they whine about why they do not have the most successful business. They complain that the general public just don't understand them, they don't appreciate their brilliance. I urge you, if you fall into this category, if you are really good at what you do, learn about marketing. Learn the formulas. There is no trickery. There are laws, rules and formulas. I look at it more like psychology of peoples buying behaviour. Great marketing will compliment the most talented and creative person to give them explosive results. I am intrigued by what triggers people's response when they make a decision to purchase something. I am impressed when I see businesses pull great talent together with an effective marketing campaign.

But my customers tell me they want the marketing trickery exposed. So here goes...

People buy on emotion

What is it that stirs your customers' emotions the most? The big ones are FEAR and GREED. What keeps them awake in bed at night worrying? What makes their heart sing with joy? If you can find that trigger, you can push that button and solve the problem for them with your goods or service.

Scarcity gets action

When you give your customers an offer in your marketing campaign, it has to have a time limit. Better still, limited stock or limited places available. Scarcity can also create urgency. They need to make a decision now. The offer is only available now. They may miss out, if they don't make a decision now.

You can also use a formula called "take away selling" where you actually tell them they can't have it, because it's only for your exclusive members. Stand back and watch how bad they want it. If you want to sell something right now, create some scarcity. Incidentally, I am not suggesting you lie. You may only have limited stock or limited places.

This formula will get a reaction from people, when you let them know.

People love to think they got a bargain

They want "Bragging Rights" on what a bargain they got. This is where the principle about giving free stuff away is so popular. The other principle is writing the price down, and then putting a huge black mark through it.

As a business owner you don't have to sell your goods at recommended retail price. You may have negotiated a better deal with your supplier, but the price you write on the ticket, is the price you could have charged. Your customer thinks they got a bargain and you still make a profit. I don't see this as trickery, as some do. If you are happy with the price you paid, why is it relevant if the business still made a profit?

Some numbers work better than others

The rule is prime numbers seem to sell better - prices that end in prime numbers: $9.95, $29.99 or $27.95. I suppose the thinking is they are just under a significant number. I can't always explain the reasoning to this one, but I know it works.

I will take a price up to a prime number, rather than down. I have particular success with 7 and it seems to be used a lot in business books.

Position, position, position

Certain positions work better in marketing. "Extra" items on a menu are strategically placed in the most viewed section, to get you to add on to your purchase. There are impulse items on the check-out counters, to remind you that you might have forgotten to buy a chocolate bar! The highest profit or most popular drinks displayed in the drink fridge at the gas station are at eye level. The less popular or less profitable ones are hard to reach. The same thing happens on the supermarket shelf. The high traffic areas of stores have impulse items or high profit items in them.

When writing a letter, the P.S. at the bottom is ALWAYS read, so it is suggested you put your key message in the P.S. There are many more examples I could mention. These things are what I consider "Good Real Estate". Use them wisely.

SOME FINAL SECRETS FOR WOMEN IN BUSINESS

Mentors, masterminds & support networks

Now I've never been an alcoholic, but I do know that one of the first steps in the 12-step programme is something like "realize you can't do it on your own". It is possible in business, you could do it on your own, but the fast track way would be to get some help. You may have to pay for the help, but not always.

If you want to fast track your knowledge in business find a mentor or mastermind group. Most problems in business happen right across the board. You'd be really surprised at the similarities and solutions that can come out of discussing your business with like-minded people.

I was involved in a Mentoring Programme run by the Government for women in 2000 and it was brilliant. We formed a mastermind group after the programme finished.

The women I met, I now count as some of my closest friends. I used to joke that it felt like our mastermind group was a therapy session for women in business. We sometimes had women in tears explaining the challenges they were facing and how overwhelmed they were.

It was wonderful to have so many women around me that genuinely wanted me to succeed. It was a nurturing environment, with some real hard-arse business minds. What a combination! The power of the mastermind group would almost always come up with solutions to any problem. We've solved issues relating to staff, husbands, stock levels, the tax department and even finding a good cleaner. Now that's a truly unique women's experience.

There are many business-networking organizations that you can join and find like-minded business people. I am involved in several women in business type organizations. I really enjoy meeting new people and discussing business, but networking and small talk is not for everyone. If that is the case for you, finding a mentor could be the answer.

If there is someone you particularly admire in business, ask him or her if they will mentor you. If not, get in touch with the government department relating to business. Many have mentoring programmes which are free and they hook you up with a mentor who can assist you with your business.

If this is still not for you, you may like to try learning at your own pace. A mentor can be as close as the website or your local bookshop. There is so much information available free on-line, you just have to look. I am constantly reading books on business, marketing, self-development and parenting. I read them when I want to – there is no pressure to read at certain times. You may want to look at madamemarketing. com.au, which runs an on-line coaching programme ideal for people who want to work at their own pace.

Since this book is really for women in, or planning to be in, business, I feel I should mention a few other support networks. A famous Australian female politician once said. "A cleaner is cheaper than a divorce". I know the statistics on couples arguing over money are high, but I'd love to see the statistics on couples arguing over cleaning the house!

Even when we couldn't afford a cleaner, we got one, every two weeks. I have girlfriends who love cleaning, so it is no chore for them. For me, it is.

Your support network at home might take the form of an ironing lady, getting healthy meals delivered, gardening, pool cleaner or even a dog walker. I find I function better when there is order in my life. This is back to one of the fast-track principles of knowing what you are good at, and delegating other duties to someone who works at a cheaper rate than you.

I am also very lucky to have a support network of other mums. I met them all through a baby clinic many years ago and we are all still friends over 10 years later. None of them are in business, but these mums, over the years, have helped me with parenting advice, babysitting and providing a shoulder to cry on. I always joke I will never make 'mother of the year', but these women make me realize that just because I'm a woman in business, doesn't mean I love my children any less.

They also make me realize, that as mums, we all make mistakes, just like any human being. It doesn't matter if you are a businesswoman or a stay at home mum. We can sit around and laugh at and with each other, as well as learn from each other.

Back off!

It felt like it was a scene from the Matrix. I was in full flight running and what I thought was helping turned out to be interfering when the presenter yelled at me from the stage "BACK OFF Sharon". My body sorted of twisted mid-flight and I seamed to be flying at 90 degrees, inches from the ground. I was helping out at an entrepreneur's boot camp and when I got back to the other side of the room, all my mates were sitting around laughing.

Now you think the lesson I must have learnt that day was to not interfere in other people's business. Well, yes I did learn that, but the most important lesson I learnt was the power in those words "BACK OFF".

During the boot camp, one of my responsibilities was to umpire the volleyball games. The majority of the players were men. I often complained to the other support crew, who were also mainly men that the men didn't listen to me because I was a woman. I explained that these were strong alpha male types, and not use to a woman in authority, so they questioned all my decisions and yelled at me, if they didn't like my calls. The men in the support team were not having the same problem. The whole purpose of the volleyball game was to teach the similarity between the game and real life business. There were great lessons on working as a team, coping with pressure and competition. Then my mate Chen said to me, that if that's what I believed to be the truth, it was, and he asked me if it was the same for me in business. I was looking at it like a victim. I was not taking any responsibility for how I was handling the situation. So I asked, "Well what can I do"? "Stand up to them, he said use Brad's expression, tell them to Back-off".

The next morning, whistle in hand. I called the game with authority and control. I ignored sniggering remarks from players and they soon stopped saying them. Then I had this six-foot guy challenge me on a call. Came right up to my face and yelled at me that I was wrong. I said in a firm loud voice, "Back off, I've called the shot, get on with it". He backed right down and went on with the game. I was shaking in my boots but thrilled at my newfound confidence.

I have many female friends in business and I feel this is one of our biggest obstacles in running a business and managing our time. It's the difference between being a victim of circumstances and being in charge of your own life and your business. A victim of circumstance doesn't take responsibility, denies there is any problem, blames everyone else for the situation and is not accountable for her actions.

It's everyone else's fault. It's the competition, it's the staff, it's the weather, it's the economy, it's my family, it's my upbringing, it's time, it's money, the list is huge, and frankly, I've used them all. You will slowly notice a pattern here. As a victim you suddenly have no control over your destiny. Anyone can make you do whatever he or she wants. You don't have to say no, you just do what others tell you. If you run a business and have a family, this is a fast road to misery and a breakdown.

A woman in charge of her life and business looks at situations differently. She takes responsibility, learns from mistakes, is accountable and takes ownership of situations that challenge her.

My thing was being bullied. Wanting to be popular, I didn't like to say no or appear rude. I have been bullied, particularly in business. I have had people be rude to be me and push me into things I didn't want to do. I've given in to pushy sales people because I thought they just wouldn't take no for an answer. I've let staff dictate their conditions, which were sometimes better than mine!

I've let customers talk me down so much that I wasn't making any money and I still sold to them. I've blamed the competition for taking business away from me, rather than working out how to get it back.

I don't anymore and I urge you not to. From family to business, you know what values, people and things are most important to you. When someone threatens that, like a mother lion protecting her young, tell them to 'BACK OFF."

Stress busters

Let's face it, life can get stressful. Add a business and motherhood on top and you can really have some up and down days. What I have learnt over the years is you HAVE TO LEARN TO COPE WITH STRESS. Find some tricks to cope and use them like a bag of resources you would in anything else you do.

Firstly I like to call stress, pressure. "I'm under a little pressure right now", that way I feel it's only temporary and it usually is.

Next, you have to look after yourself physically and mentally so that when life throws you a "curly one" you can handle it. I look at my stress management levels like MONEY IN THE BANK. When life turns on a bit of pressure and my stress management levels are in the black, I can handle almost anything that is thrown at me - from family to work. When my stress levels are in THE RED, it doesn't take much to crack me.

The thing is, by managing my physical and mental wellbeing I can keep "on top" most of the time. For me I find I am rejuvenated by a massage, meditation, a casual lunch with friends, a day at the beach, talking to a good friend who loves you just the way you are, taking my vitamins, drinking plenty of water, an afternoon sleep on a weekend, an early morning walk with some motivating music, a drink on a Friday night. But everyone is different. What gets you back in the black? You really need to learn this about yourself. You need to know what tops up your stress levels. I have tried to find a balance between things that don't cost any money and things that are a little treat.

I'm a bit hormonal right now!

Everything that happens in a women's body happens in a cycle. This is completely different to a man's body. But it is not our fault, we are just built that way. For that reason we have to look after ourselves differently. I am aware some women have problems around their period time and hormones. All the related and varied symptoms that women experience around this time can have a huge impact on our confidence levels, on our performance, energy, and our ability to succeed in business. In some ways because of this, we can also sabotage our success.

I personally don't have a huge problem with this (although my husband may disagree!) But I know many women in business struggle with their moods and energy as a result of hormonal imbalances. I personally can get irritable around that time of the month. I know I have over-reacted or possibly said something in anger, I shouldn't have said. I have sometimes temporarily damaged business and staff relationships by this. I believe many women's hormones can make them feel overwhelmed, irritable or extra emotional.

It can put women in business on the back foot when we are playing with the big boys in business. If you feel it is a problem or is holding back your success, getting help dealing with the symptoms associated with hormonal imbalances, can free up your energy levels to be the best you can be.

I have organised a free audio interview with women's health expert Gabriela Rosa on "How Within 27 Days You Can Quickly And Easily Stop Hormones Sabotaging Your success and start taking back control of your future. Valued at over $247. If this is an issue for you, Go to Madamemarketing.com.au to get the free audio.

My thoughts on mother guilt

It's not about perfection, but self-correction.

Repeat after me: Guilt is a wasted emotion. It achieves nothing. If you are feeling guilt, try and fix the situation. If you can't you must 'accept the things you cannot change and move on'. Yes, but the bottom line is, sometimes I still feel guilty.

I have found the person that gives you the hardest time about guilt is yourself. The pressure you feel is often self-inflicted. So, be nice to yourself.

I know there are plenty of books written about work and life balance. It's all about discipline and structure. I try and do most of it, but at times, I slip up. I've missed business commitments because I'm distracted with my children or I've missed mother commitments because I'm distracted at work. There are times when the business needs me more than my family and times my family needs me more than the business. For me it's not about balance. It's about imbalance. It's about making a decision regarding the difficult situations as they come along.

It's about going with the flow.

What I have found that works for me is finding the resources to help keep you on top of it. I feel a tidy house keeps me better organised. So a cleaner was a great investment. Having said that, I will never win an award for tidiest house of the year. My house is clean, but not always tidy. I don't let it get to me as I feel there are more important things to do. I have found giving the children small jobs to do on a daily basis, helps.

I am a morning person, so getting up before everyone else and squeezing a little paperwork in has been a good way for me to keep on top of things. I am also very guarded with my time. I don't have long gossipy phone calls unless I'm driving (hands-free). I don't particularly read those emails that promise me bad luck if I don't reply to them. I often just delete them. When I am out with friends or family I try to be totally focused on the moment and enjoy it.

When my children were very young, I only worked part-time. Business life accelerated once they went to school and that was great.

I was really ready. I was never going to be a 'stay at home' mum. I need more stimulation and as much as my children have taught me patience, I know I don't have enough to be a full time mum. Being a mum in business, there was no maternity leave, no getting paid to have the day off because the children are sick. The great thing though is the flexibility it has given me to have time off, when I want to.

I know I cannot get back the days I missed with my children, but I truly feel the days I had and have with my children, I cherish. I now work school hours the majority of the time. I make up my workload when my husband is around or the children are asleep. I've learned to become a lot more efficient with my time. It's very precious to me and it's rare that I waste it.

I also know a lot of mothers in business. Many tell me they regretted working full time when their children were really young, but felt there was no option. The bottom line is if you are a mum in business, then it's your decision. There are always ways to make what you want work. Full time nannies and full time day care are another option. Some options may cost more money, they may delay your big plans, and you may miss out on more sleep than normal. Nonetheless, there are always options, if that is what you want.

If you are unsure and looking for some guidance, from my experience and other mothers I know, try part-time. It's easier to take on more, than get rid of a huge workload. There are many options that can fast track your business after your children have gone to school. If you do choose to work part-time, why not enjoy educating yourself with books or CD's, so when you do have more time, you'll know exactly what to do.

Hey, try a little imbalance, and enjoy it!

Working with your husband

"If you really want to grow and improve yourself go and do a personal development course. If you want to up the ante a little bit more, get into a relationship with an equal. And if that isn't fast enough, have children. And if you want to speed it up even more get into your own business with them"
Mary Blackburn

I was doing a fabulous course on the power of the mind, run by my good friends Paul and Mary Blackburn, when Mary came up with this great quote.

She said if you want to challenge and improve yourself and

your thinking, go on a self-development course or the other option is to marry your equal. They have to be your equal to challenge you and move you forward. If you want to accelerate your 'learning" go into business with them; if you really want to accelerate your learning, have babies with them.

If you are going to work with your husband, I really feel one of the secrets here is the personality test and the job descriptions. Be very clear about what you expect from each other. Paul and Mary Blackburn are one of the leading educators in Australia in finding your mind blockages to success. I have personally had consultations with them and have attended several seminars where Paul has spoken. As you get more and more successful you may start to challenge your internal belief systems. Paul helped me with some easy to use techniques that helped me and continue to help me break through my own limitations.

> *If you feel like you are sabotaging your own success,*
> *it may be worthwhile checking out Paul and*
> *Mary Blackburn's website.*
> *Go to www.blockagebusters.com/mmarketing*

Time to talk

Every week my husband and I try to sit down and talk about the week in business that has passed. We have another friend in business who makes fun of us doing this. "A business meeting at home" yeah right!

What do you really get up to? But just because we are both working in the business, doesn't mean we get to communicate the best during the week. We often find we are blurting things at each other as we get ready for bed or getting dinner ready with the children. It's not an optimum time to relay important information about your business. We occasionally go to the local coffee shop and make it a little fun.

We have some other friends in business and they have their weekly meeting on Sunday morning on the deck. My friend makes croissants, fruit and good coffee and she and her husband discuss how the business is travelling and what things are coming up. It's something they both look forward to and it gives them clarity for the week. They have teenage girls, so it doesn't cut into family time or work time.

For us Friday mornings works best. Our children are at school and we usually only meet for 1½ hours. We find it really gives us clarity as to what needs to be done and where we are both up to. We also find when we don't do it, our week is all over the place and we don't get as much done.

So I suppose taking 90 minutes out of the week for us is well worth it.

We also like to have some structure to the meeting. We discuss the most important challenges facing the business: cash flow, stock, staff, that sort of thing. We 'think tank' how we can fix it or if we can't come up with a resolution, we work out who we can call to get the information. My husband also prepares the financials for the meeting. Just something rough, so we know how we are travelling: cash at bank, turnover, debtors, creditors, any problems with late payers etc.

The meetings I enjoy most are our strategic meetings. We discuss how we can afford to build a mezzanine floor or how can we afford another sales rep, that sort of thing. Then we go through the numbers, what return on our investment we expect.

Our Agenda looks something like this.

Firstly we: Synchronise Diaries, what are our time commitments with work, family and each other this week.

Don't forget the mother-in-law's coming for dinner!

Then we discuss:

- Business;
- Family; and
- Investments.

Meditation or motion?

Just running around at full speed is not the answer. Well, it was not for me anyway. When I did this, I often felt overwhelmed and resentful. Learning to meditate was one of the best things I did for my sanity. It has helped me keep focused and even-tempered in stressful situations.

Being in business means there is usually some sort of drama or mini drama daily. Well I used to think so. That sort of thing doesn't happen so much anymore. I am a lot calmer and can handle any daily mishaps that come my way. So many little things used to irritate me before I learnt to meditate. The thing is, it took me a good two years to get good at it and hundreds of dollars in finding the right type of way to learn.

I found listening to a guided meditation the best to start with. These are CD's that talk you through a beautiful sort of story as they gently relax you. This is a great way to start and the CD's are available on-line or in bookstores. The problem with these is when you play them a few times the repetition becomes boring. I finally learnt to meditate on my own with the help of some wonderful teachers.

This book is all about fast tracking you to success, so I have discovered a fast track way to learn this skill. I believe meditation is a fabulous skill to learn, especially if you find you can be a little moody or anxious. The latest technique I have tried is "Holosync Meditations". They are CD's of beautiful music that can take as little as 30 minutes.

The magic of them is they are subliminal. You don't actually hear what is being said, but there are some vibration sounds that are very soothing, as well as rain falling and gentle chimes. It is all scientific and I'm no scientist, but I can tell you for me, they have been great. There are apparently ideal ways to listen to them, but I have listened to them in bed and drifted off to sleep for a few minutes and still felt fabulous afterward.

FREE BONUS GIFT

Meditate.com.au has kindly offered to send our readers a free report and free sample holosync meditation CD. Valued at over $37.

Go to www.meditate.com/mmarketing

TIME TO TAKE ACTION

The difference between you now, and you in 5 years time, is the people you meet and the books you read.

I hope you have enjoyed this book and that it has given you some insight into how to make the journey faster and more enjoyable on your road to business and financial success. I have included some books below that have changed my life. I enjoy reading books on business and marketing. I could have included a long list of books that are usually at the back of business books, but as this book is about fast tracking information for busy women, I have included some books that I feel are life changing. The information is clear and concise and the books are easy to read. I've also tried to explain why they are so good.

I will make one final note on fast tracking this part of your journey as well. After all, let's face it, we all know we should read more of these types of books, but who has the time.

Right! When I do get to them, I enjoy reading these types of books, but I have found an easier way to do it. It's my little "temple of learning" or what some might refer to as a "Motor Vehicle".

I would buy more business books as audio books than anything else. I figure I spend at least ten hours a week in my car and apart from catching up on phone calls; this has been my best use of time. If you looked at it over the last five years, I suppose I've almost done the equivalent time as a university degree. If you know you should, and you want to, but time is limited, I would suggest you "listen" to the ones you really want to know about first.

Books you should read

Fast track Books that changed my life:

Think and Grow Rich

By Napoleon Hill

This book for me was about getting your attitude right. It also gives a great insight into how the rich think and why they do what they do. I have read it several times and always get something new from it.

Rich Dad, Poor Dad

By Robert Kiyosaki

Compares two "Fathers" and their attitudes to money and life. One is academic and conservative, the other more streetwise and goal orientated. It's told like a story and is really easy reading but with some great messages.

Your Right to be Rich

By Mal Emery

A no "BS" account of how to make money fast in business with real life examples.

The Cashflow Quadrant

By Robert Kiyosaki

This books explains to you how you can get out of the rat race of life and how you got their in the first place – really great strategies that I have used and have worked. I still refer to this book to make sure I'm on the right track.

The E Myth

By Michael Gerber

"E" is for Entrepreneurial. This book showed me how and why to systemise my businesses so I didn't have to work in them to make money. If you are exhausted in your business, read this one first.

The One Minute Millionaire

By Mark Victor Hansen & Robert Allen

I have never enjoyed a business book as much as this. It is the first time I have bought a second copy, before finishing the copy I had. The reason being my husband and I were both reading it at the same time! It's told like a story, with some amazing messages and inspiration.

Billionaires in Training

By Brad Sugars

This book explained to me the processes you go through to become better and bigger in business. It gives really good advice on how to grow businesses, as this is Brad's speciality.

Instant Cash Flow

By Brad Sugars

This used to be like my Cash flow bible. When I just couldn't work out what was going wrong, I use to turn to this book and find a dozen answers straight away to boost my cash flow.

Secrets of Marketing Experts Exposed

By Dale Beaumont

Interviews with some of Australia's leading marketing experts – and I'm one of them!

The Richest Man in Babylon

By George Glasson

Firstly, this is only a little book, so quick to read. It explains how just tweaking little things with money will give you financial freedom. Based on one of the richest civilisations in the world. Really simple to follow instructions that work.

The 7 Habits of Highly Effective People

By Steven Covey

This man is brilliant and his books are amazing. However, I find them a little heavy to read. What is wonderful though is this book is available on audio CD. It's the sort of CD you can listen to over and over again and hear a different message each time. Besides I figure what better way to learn such important effective habits than by having them constantly repeated to you.

The people you should meet

If you search for local women in business networking groups you are sure to find some really interesting people that will change your life. Alternatively there are some great business referral groups and community groups. If you are feeling a little isolated or in need of some positive support, I urge you to try to contact your local group. I also urge you to stop hanging around people that make you feel miserable. Some people you meet give you energy, revitalize you, nurture you, uplift you. Others suck the energy out and leave you flat and exhausted. If you can't keep away from people who make you feel bad, try and limit your contact with them as much as possible. Surrounding yourself with the people who make you feel good, will help you achieve success faster.

I urge you to surround yourself with winners to fast track your success. People who live their lives consistent with the values and beliefs you have or wish to acquire. It's ok to sometimes be out of your comfort zone. Be the observer and be yourself. See what you can learn by listening and observing.

Exclusive Limited FREE Offer
The Most Amazing FREE Gift Ever valued at $697

Yes! I can't wait to take you up on your amazing FREE offer where I get the complete CD & DVD set of Mal Emery and Madame Marketing's own marketing wisdom PLUS a selection of revealing interviews with the world's most incredible Millionaire Making entrepreneurs, including....

1. Breakthrough Marketing Strategies and Tactics PLUS 6 ADVANCED Marketing Secrets DVD.

2. The 7 Most Important Changes, Trends & Opportunities in Info Marketing Today Featuring Dan Kennedy.

3. The Ultimate Info-Marketing Shortcut: Bill Glazer's A-to-Z Info Business Blueprint for Info-Marketers.

4. "How to Master the Single Critical Skill that Pours Money into Your Bank Account, Day and Night... Almost like Magic" featuring Yanik Silver.

5. Mal Emery interviews Harry S. Dent, the author of "The Great Boom Ahead", about his predictions for the future of business and investing in stocks, shares and real estate.

6. Mal Emery interviews DC Cordova - DC reveals her and Robert Kiyosaki's Business Success Model - Masters, Niche, Leverage, Aligned Team, Synergy and Results.

7. Interview with Chris Payne: "The 4 Lies Your Mind Tells You Which Can Create Sadness, Frustration and Anxiety and Hold You Back From the Riches You Deserve."

8. Interview with Ted Nicholas: "World Renowned Author, Copywriter, Self-Publisher, Public Speaker and Direct Marketing Expert."

9. Interview with Paul Hartunian: "Professional Speaking on Your Feet" – famous for selling the Brooklyn Bridge.

10. Dr. Gene Landrum "Spills the beans on the Laws of Entrepreneurship that he has explored through the lives and achievements of 12 of the world's most eminent entrepreneurs."

11. Wonderful Web Women interviews Madame Marketing on how to create a "Mastermind Group" that get's results and ALSO reveals her negotiating strategies to get a better deal 9 out of 10 times, and NEVER PAY RETAIL AGAIN.

12. Interview with Madame Marketing where she uncovers the 'BREAK-THROUGH MILLION DOLLAR PRODUCT" that generated her business over $1 million dollars and how you can adapt it to sell it in your business too.

PLUS you get to "Test Drive" for a full 3 months the "Madame Marketing's Closed Door Secrets" for members only, where she "pulls back the curtain on what actually works in Marketing with her exclusive on-line coaching programme. Email her any-time with your marketing challenges. See where she reveals the STUFF THAT WORKS! Have your own Marketing Coach as close as your computer, ready to give you the fast track secrets, or bounce ideas off. After a full 3 months FREE, unless directed otherwise we will continue to send you the "closed door marketing secrets" and give you access to Madame Marketing via email and charge your credit card $47.

Of course if you don't wish to continue to access "Madame Marketing's Closed Door Secrets" or have your own on-line Marketing Coach, simply tell us by phone on 1800 247 835 or email: info@madamemarketing.com and we will cancel your membership immediately and not charge your credit card another cent. No questions asked!

Please note you will be charged a one off postage and handling fee of $15.

Name:_____Date:_____

Address:_____

Suburb/State/Postcode:_____

Phone:_____Fax:_____Mobile:_____

Email Address:_____

Credit Card number: _ _ _ _ / _ _ _ _ / _ _ _ _ / _ _ _ _ Exp date _ _ / _ _

Signature: _____card 3-4 digit security code_____

Simply FAX THIS FORM TO AUSTRALIA:- 02 433 33493

DEDICATION & ACKNOWLEDGEMENT

My first impulse was to dedicate this book to my husband Jim and my beautiful children, Isaac and Dana. They give me their unconditional love and support, which in turn enables be to be the best person I can be. They all have a wonderful sense of humour and I value the amazing bond of "team Tieman" that we have created. I admire Jim's sense of being so grounded and calm and love having that influence in a sometimes-mad world. I love Isaac's determination and persistence. He will always be a winner in life. I love Dana's amazingly inquisitive mind and her gentle loving nature. She is a pleasure to be around. They know that I am grateful for them and love them in my life, because I tell them daily.

I must also give thanks to my Dad for guiding me towards business. I always enjoy our talks and I thank him for his inspiration. Thank you to my Mum for her generosity. Thank you to Kaye for her support. Thank you to Brad for his wonderful sense of humour and loyalty.

Thank you to the Tieman clan for welcoming me into the family with such love and warmth. To Oma and Opa who are the most generous and loving in-laws anyone could ever hope for.

The saying goes, "the difference between you now and you in five years is the people you meet and the books you read." For that reason, I must mention two mentors that changed my life. Brad Sugars had the guts to run entrepreneur boot camps and generously give his knowledge and secrets to wealth. I was fortunate enough to attend twice and meet him. His books have inspired me and I am forever grateful for the generosity of the knowledge he gave me.

Of course I would have to mention my great mentor Mal Emery, who was the first person to stand up to me and say "Sharon, just shut up and listen". I am very grateful for that, because when I did, a world of opportunity and knowledge poured from him generously. When I think of Mal, I think of generosity, inspiration with a bull dogged business mind under the disguise of style and grace.

His knowledge on marketing and business is cutting edge. To this day my jaw still drops when he is explaining some business success secrets he has exposed. When people say, you don't know what you don't know, I think of what Mal Emery has taught me.

One of the quotes on my office wall is "surround yourself with people who expect more of you, than you do of yourself." So for that reason I should thank Dr. Chen Tay. He is an unreasonable friend, who pushes me beyond my limits. When you are successful, you need people like Chen who challenge you. When I have been feeling whiney and full of self pity, usually over something minor, a quick phone call to Chen is all that is needed to tell me to pull my head in and get on with it. He is a one of a kind unique friend.

Thank you also to Clifford Fairbrass for nicknaming me "Madame Marketing". The first nickname I've actually liked.

Thankyou to Glenn & Julie Stewart of Davis and Stewart Accountants. I'm so grateful to have you both on our team and your genuine interest in wanting me to be a success.

Thank you to Paul Buckingham for believing in me enough to interview me in his audio business mentor program – twice.

Thank you to the amazing businesswomen of W.I.N. on the Central Coast especially to Carolyn, Kerry, Anne, Sandra and Lynn. They are my mastermind group! Their group knowledge, friendship, support and energy has accelerated me in life. I am forever grateful to have met them.

Thankyou to my dear friend Bec Fraser, who stepped up to the plate when this book seemed to be falling apart. With a 6 month old and a multi-million dollar business herself, she got me back on track and to the publisher.

To my mothers group "M.I.A". Donna, Natasha, Wendy, Suzanne, Anita & Michelle. If a child is to be raised by a village, I choose this lot to raise my children! They support me, inspire me and challenge me.

Thank you for being such loyal good friends.

To my buddies Rosco, Kaz, Deanne, Leo, Mel, Matt, & Coges. They are my longest and dearest friends. If they still love me after all this time, then that's truly unconditional love! Thank you.

Thank you also to my staff over the years. I have really been blessed with some fantastic and supportive people, some of whom I still call friends.

This is probably the longest dedication for any book, but one of the lessons in life I have learnt is to be grateful. So in a real sense I dedicate this book as a tribute to all those people. I am very grateful for all the amazing people in my life.

There is one last person I would like to acknowledge. It's YOU. You have made the decision to pick up this book in the first place and take the time to read it to the last chapter. This tells me you are serious about your future. It will be people like you who are serious about the future of women in business that will change the future.

It will be you who will show people, through your success that you can enjoy business and a family. It will be people like you who are not afraid to stand up and be brilliant; a brilliant businesswoman.

So I dedicate this book to you:

Brilliant Business Woman

_____

(Please write your name above)